THE NATIONAL GALLERY OF VICTORIA
MELBOURNE

LES PRIMITIFS FLAMANDS

I. CORPUS DE LA PEINTURE DES ANCIENS PAYS-BAS MÉRIDIONAUX AU QUINZIÈME SIÈCLE

12

PUBLICATIONS OF THE CENTRE NATIONAL DE RECHERCHES "PRIMITIFS FLAMANDS"

I. CORPUS DE LA PEINTURE DES ANCIENS PAYS-BAS MÉRIDIONAUX AU QUINZIÈME SIÈCLE. II. RÉPERTOIRE DES PEINTURES FLAMANDES DU QUINZIÈME SIÈCLE. III. CONTRIBUTIONS À L'ÉTUDE DES PRIMITIFS FLAMANDS.

URSULA HOFF
Assistant Director
National Gallery of Victoria
Melbourne

and

MARTIN DAVIES
Director
National Gallery
London

THE NATIONAL GALLERY
OF VICTORIA

MELBOURNE

American Distributor:

Wittenborn and Company

1018 Madison Ave., New York, N. Y. 10021

BRUSSELS

MCMLXXI

TABLE OF CONTENTS

FOREWORD

This volume covering the only Flemish primitive paintings in Australasian public collections, was proposed by the late Dr. Paul Coremans during my visit to the *Centre National* in 1956.

The preparation of the text would have been impossible without the help of Mr. Martin Davies, now Director of the London National Gallery, who agreed to act as co-author for the entries on Memlinc (No. 134), Marmion (No. 133) and the Triptych (No. 131), though he had then not seen any of the originals; owing to gracious invitations issued in 1969 by the city of Bruges through Dr. Janssens de Bisthoven, Mr. Davies and I were able together to inspect the Triptych during its presence at the *Exposition Primitifs Flamands Anonymes* at the Groeninge Museum (June-September 1969). I am deeply indebted to Mr. Davies for his co-operation, which involved many patient revisions of the text, and for consulting sources not available in Australian libraries.

The photographs of Nos. 131, 133, 134 were made in Melbourne. Ritter Jeppesen Pty. Ltd. carried out the black and white prints, the Ektachrome (pl. LXXVII A) and the infra-red prints. The x-rays of these pictures were made by the Commonwealth X-ray Laboratories in Melbourne.

The Ince Blundell Madonna (No. 132) is the only painting here which has been examined in Brussels, on the occasion of the exhibition *L'art flamand dans les collections britanniques* (Bruges, August-September 1956). The examination was undertaken in conjunction with the London National Gallery and the Institut royal du Patrimoine artistique in Brussels (IRPA).

Using the facilities of the IRPA (Director, the late Dr. P. Coremans, Director a.i., Mr. R. V. Sneyers and Chief Restorer, Mr. A. Philippot) the Institut undertook to study the physical, microchemical and technical aspects of No. 132, while Mr. Martin Davies, then Deputy Keeper of the London National Gallery, carried out a stylistic and documentary analysis. Mr. F. I. G. Rawlins, then Deputy Keeper and Scientific Adviser to the Trustees of the London National Gallery, examined certain special points and in particular carried out a chromo-photographic analysis of the 'transparent layer.' Mr. Sneyers, with the assistance of Mr. Philippot, has been so good as to supply the text of C. *Physical Characteristics* using as a basis the report of 14.XI.1958 of Dr. Paul Coremans, Messrs. Philippot and Sneyers, and the report dated 15.V.58 furnished by Mr. F. I. G. Rawlins. All the photography for No. 132 was taken at the IRPA.

The first tests of solubility and the first removals of overpainting were made in November 1957 in the presence of Mr. Eric Westbrook, Director of the National Gallery of Victoria. Mr. Davies was present during major stages of examination and cleaning in December 1957 and February and April 1958, and Mr. Rawlins in March 1958. Sections of Mr. Davies' report appear in Notice 132. For other sections it was more convenient to write the comments myself, naturally taking his findings into account in the right places of the entry. I wish to record my indebtedness to the late Professor Erwin Panofsky for his exposition of the Brussels findings; to the late Professor Ludwig Baldass and to Dr. Otto Pächt who both generously gave of their time to discuss the problems connected with No. 132.

Ursula HOFF

ACKNOWLEDGEMENTS

The authors wish to thank the Committee of the *Centre* for their patience and encouragement and the Council of Trustees of the National Gallery of Victoria and its Director, Mr. Eric Westbrook, for generous permission to study and to publish the works in their Gallery.

The following have given valuable help in the preparation of this volume:

With the kind agreement of Professor Dr. H. Gerson, then Director of the *Rijksbureau voor Kunsthistorische Documentatie* at The Hague, the archives of the late M. J. Friedländer were consulted.

Much help was given by Mr. John Harthan, and the Library of the Victoria and Albert Museum, London.

For assistance with special research problems the authors are particularly indebted to Mme Veronee-Verhaegen of the *Centre* who assisted with problems of Iconography, and to Mlle Micheline Sonkes, Scientific Secretary of the *Centre*, whose aid at all stages of the project has been invaluable.

For information of various kinds our thanks are here recorded to the following: Señor Don Juan Ainaud de Lasarte, Director General, Catalonian Art Museum, Barcelona; Professor K. Bauch, formerly University of Freiburg im Breisgau, Germany; Dr. K. G. Boon, Director, Print Room, Rijksmuseum, Amsterdam; Professor J. Bruyn, University of Amsterdam; Mr. Lorne Campbell, at the time of the University of Manchester; Mr. Staffan Cullberg of the National Museum, Stockholm; Dr. Hannah Dornik-Eger of the Austrian Museum for Applied Art, Vienna; Dr. Rosalie B. Green, Index of Christian Art, Princeton University; Mr. A. Lawalrée, Chef de Département at the Jardin botanique de l'État, Brussels; Mr. David Lawrance, Chief Conservator, National Gallery of Victoria, Melbourne; Dr. Ulrich Middeldorf, formerly Director, Kunsthistorisches Institut, Florence; Miss Dorothy Miner, of the Walters Art Gallery, Baltimore; Professor Peter Murray, former Witt Librarian, The Courtauld Institute of Arts, London; Dr. F. Mütherich, Zentralinstitut für Kunstgeschichte, Munich; the late Mr. Franz Philipp, Fine Arts Department, University of Melbourne; Dr. M. Poch-Kalous, Director, Gemäldegalerie der Akademie der bildenden Künste, Vienna; Mr. D. J. Stevens, Director, Commonwealth X-ray and Radium Laboratory, Melbourne; Professor Roger Van Schoute, University of Louvain; Dr. Stephan Waetzold, Generaldirektor, Staatliche Museen, Berlin; Mr. Christopher White, formerly Assistant Keeper, Department of Prints and Drawings, British Museum, London; Mr. J. Willis, Assistant Government Botanist, The Royal Botanical Gardens and National Herbarium, Melbourne; the late Professor Dr. F. Winkler, Berlin.

Ursula HOFF, Martin DAVIES

EXPLANATIONS

Classification of the Pictures in the Corpus

The painters whose works are studied in the Corpus may be *anonymous*, or be known by *name*, or else by a *distinguishing title*. The pictures are therefore arranged in one of the three following categories:

ANONYMOUS

GROUP followed by the (sometimes abbreviated) name of the painter (e.g. GROUP EYCK, GROUP MEMLINC)

MASTER OF ... (e.g. MASTER OF THE S. URSULA LEGEND). If a painting is the work of more than one master, it will be classified under ANONYMOUS.

The alphabetical order is followed in the last two categories. The pictures thus classified are given two *Corpus numbers*. Example:

No. 134: GROUP MEMLINC (15), *The Man of Sorrows in the Arms of the Virgin*.

This means: No. 134 of the Corpus, group of works associated with Memlinc, fifteenth work studied in this group. This classification has been adopted for practical reasons. It does not imply acceptance of the attribution.

Left and right

The terms *Left* (l.) and *Right* (r.) are used for the spectator's left and right, unless the context clearly implies the contrary.

Measurements

The measurements are given both in inches and in centimetres; the order is height × width × thickness. As the shape of ancient panels is generally irregular, the measurements are approximate.

Indications of Scale

1 : 1   means: photograph (and plate) the actual size of the original.

M 2×, 5×, 10× ... means: macrophotograph (and plate) twice, five times, ten times ... the size of the original.

M 1 ½× approx. means: macrophotograph (and plate) approximately one and half the size of the original.

A. CLASSIFICATION IN THE CORPUS

No. 131: ANONYMOUS (13), *THE TRIPTYCH WITH THE MIRACLES OF CHRIST*

B. IDENTIFYING REFERENCES

Master of the Legend of S. Catherine, and others.
The Multiplication of the Loaves and Fishes; The Marriage at Cana; The Repose on the Flight to Egypt; The Raising of Lazarus; S. Peter.
No. 1247/3 in the Catalogue of *European Paintings before Eighteen Hundred, National Gallery of Victoria*, Melbourne, 1967 ([38] 50-55).

C. PHYSICAL CHARACTERISTICS
(15-II-66)

Form: Triptych.

Dimensions:			
Centre,	panel		$113,9 \times 83,4 \times 0,9$ cm
			$44\frac{13}{16} \times 32\frac{7}{8} \times \frac{3}{8}$ ins
	painted surface		$113 \times 82,4$ cm
			$44\frac{1}{2} \times 32\frac{7}{16}$ ins
Left wing,	panel		$113 \times 37,2 \times 1,1$ cm
			$44\frac{1}{2} \times 14\frac{5}{8} \times \frac{7}{16}$ ins
	painted surface, obverse		$112,2 \times 35,6$ cm
			$44\frac{3}{16} \times 14\frac{1}{16}$ ins
	painted surface, reverse		$112 \times 35,3$ cm
			$44\frac{1}{8} \times 13\frac{7}{8}$ ins
Right wing,	panel		$113,3 \times 37,3 \times 1,1$ cm
			$44\frac{5}{8} \times 14\frac{11}{16} \times \frac{7}{16}$ ins
	painted surface, obverse		112×36 cm
			$44\frac{1}{8} \times 14\frac{3}{16}$ ins
	painted surface, reverse		$112 \times 35,4$ cm
			$44\frac{1}{8} \times 13\frac{15}{16}$ ins.

Protective Layer: Obverse: A thin layer of modern varnish, clear.
Reverse of the wings: A thick layer of varnish, modern, slightly coloured.
Paint Layer: In good condition; adheres well; fine craquelure. The edges of the paint show no barbe. The unpainted edges are narrow in the central panel but wider in the wings. Slight damage appears along the joints

particularly on the central panel (Pl. IX, XL and XLI) and on the inner left wing. In the latter the join runs through figs. 3 and 4 which have small repaints (Pl. XIII and XLII). Paint losses appear in the lower garments of fig. 9 (Pl. XIV).

On the reverse of the left wing there is some overpainting around the head of the Virgin. Fairly extensive repaints suggesting paint losses appear in the face of the Virgin; between her head and the halo on the r.; between the fluttering garment of the angel and the upper bunch of dates, to the r. of the church tower; white spots lie on the paint surface in that area (Pl. XXVII and XLIV). Considerable re-paints in the right hand side of the Virgin's robe and in the skirt of her blue dress. The right wing is in good preservation.

Changes in Composition: The infra-red photographs of selected areas show the presence of underdrawing in all panels.

In the central panel the drawing for heads 11 and 12 (Pl. XXXIV) reveals marked alterations. Underneath head 11 appears the outline of a young woman's face and hood, occupying a different position from the head that replaced it. The eyes of head 12 seem to have been intended to be lower down. The underdrawing here consists mainly of outlines of varying thickness.

In the left wing observe, underdrawing in figs. 2, 3, 4, 5 is also mainly linear but shows a firmer line than that in the central panel (Pl. XXXVII); outlines as well as hatching appear in the bride (Pl. XXXVI). There is a small correction in the outline of the forehead of fig. 5; the tiled floor seems to have been intended to continue further back; a correction appears at the back of the cap of fig. 3 and in the contour of the face of fig. 2 (Pl. XXXVII).

More extensive underdrawing of a markedly different style appears in the right hand panel observe; here hatching and contour lines are combined; the drawing is free and creative but changes are of a minor nature (Pl. XXXV). No changes could be observed in the areas photographed in infra-red on the reverse of the wings. In the left wing reverse, the underdrawing consists of faint outlines and hatching in the Virgin's robe (Pl. XXXVIII); in the right wing reverse the folds are lightly outlined and faint parallel shading occurs in the hands (Pl. XXXIX).

Ground: Nearly white, thin, adheres well.

Support: Oak; central panel: three members with vertical grain, and modern cradling; left wing: two members with vertical grain; right wing: one member with vertical grain.

Marks on the back: Nothing worth recording (Pl. XLVIII a).

Frame: Not original.

D. DESCRIPTION AND ICONOGRAPHY

1. *Subject*

Central panel

The early part of the story is illustrated in the middle distance, where Christ sits on a mountain, surrounded by seven disciples. One of the two disciples on the l. may be S. Philip looking at the multitude; at the extreme r., perhaps S. Andrew, who seems to be introducing a lad with five barley loaves and two small fishes (Pl. VI). The company below has sat down, the miracle has taken place, they have eaten. Four disciples are gathering up what is over in four baskets; eight further baskets with bread and fish bones are on the ground in the foreground, at the feet of S. Peter, who seems to be recognizable from his type (cf. what is said by *L. Réau, Icono-graphie de l'art chrétien*, III, *Iconographie des Saints*, Part III, Paris, 1959, p. 1083). The apostle in the middle distance on the extreme l., beardless and very young, may be S. John (*Réau, op. cit.*, Part II, 1958, p. 711). There are only eleven apostles in all (Pl. IV, V, VII).

The Miracle of the Feeding of the Five Thousand is recorded in all four Gospels: *Matthew* (XIV, 15-21), *Mark* (VI, 35-44), *Luke* (IX, 12-17), and *John* (VI, 3-13). A comparable miracle of the Feeding of Four Thousand is recorded in *Matthew* (XV, 32-38) and *Mark* (VIII, 1-9). This picture illustrates the former miracle. The Gospel accounts correspond quite closely, but some details peculiar to *John's* account (v. 3 and 9) are certainly shown in the picture. *Mark* (VI, 43) is the only evangelist who specifies the collecting of fishes as well as fragments of bread. Women and children among the multitude are mentioned only in *Matthew* (XIV, 21). It should be noted that the number of twelve apostles present is specified only in *Luke*.

Further miracles are shown in the background: on the lake side on the l., Christ heals the sick probably as related in the gospels before the main miracle, perhaps a conflation of the accounts in *Matthew* (XIV, 13-14) and *Luke* (IX, 10-11); compare *John* (VI, 2) (Pl. VII).

On the lake side on the r. Christ appears to be dismissing the multitude according to *Matthew* (XIV, 22-23) or *Mark* (VI, 45-46). Further to the r., the miracle succeeding the Feeding of the Five Thousand: the apostles have apparently entered a boat on the sea of Galilee (*Matthew* XIV, 22; *Mark* VI, 45; *John* VI, 17). Further back, Christ and S. Peter are walking on the water (*Matthew* XIV, 28-31); contrary to the gospel account, the water is calm and it is day. This miracle in this form is not related in the other gospels (Pl. VI).

In the background projecting into the water is the view of a fortified town with a large church, standing either for Capernaum as in *John* (VI, 17), or Bethsaida as in *Mark* (VI, 45), and *Luke* (IX, 10).

Above, in a circle of cloud, God is blessing; He is wearing a tiara encircled with one crown and surmounted by a cross and is holding an orb in His l. hand; faint outlines of two angels appear to His r.; there is one angel on His l. (Pl. VIII). A similar figure, not accompanied by angels, is to be found in the *Flight to Egypt*, l. wing reverse.

Certain points of iconography are peculiar in this picture. To show Christ together with some of the apostles in the middle distance is uncommon in representations earlier than 1500.

The theme of the picture here occurs occasionally in Franco-Flemish manuscript illuminations of the 14th and 15th century, differently composed. In certain manuscripts and panel paintings that are clearly earlier than the Melbourne picture Christ appears in the foreground. One case is in the retable of the *Transfiguration*, Cathedral of Barcelona, assigned to the school of the Master of S. George, dated by *Post* probably soon after 1445 (*J. Ainaud, J. Gudiol* and *F. P. Verrié, Catálogo Monumental de España, La Ciudad de Barcelona*, Madrid, 1947, II, fig. 454; *Ch. R. Post, A History of Spanish Painting*, Cambridge, Mass., II, 1930, p. 418-426). Another example occurs in the altarpiece of S. Wolfgang am Abersee, of 1471-81, by Michael Pacher (*E. Hempel, Das Werk Michael Pachers*, Vienna, 1940, pl. 66).

On the other hand, in a triptych assigned to Cornelis Engebrechtsz. of about 1520 (now Greenville, Bob Jones University), Christ blessing the bread has been placed far into the middle distance (*M. J. Friedländer, Die Alt-niederländische Malerei*, X, *Lucas van Leyden und andere holländische Meister seiner Zeit*, Berlin, 1932, pl. XXXIX).

There is in the Melbourne picture a repeated emphasis on drinking; to the r. a woman is taking water from a spring; a man approaches it with a bottle; bottles stand in between the rows of the multitude; fig. 14 is shown with a bottle raised to her lips, as is another woman to the r. of Christ. The repeated references to drinking may be compared with the inscription which occurs in the Engebrechtsz. picture referred to above on the coat of the man in the r. foreground: *"Nu eens te drin[ken]"* (now a drink is what I shoud like); though this comparison is limited by a possible comic inference there (see *F. Dülberg, The Feeding of the Five Thousand, by Cornelis Engebrechtszoon*, in *The Burlington Magazine* (London), Vol. XLIII, 1923, p. 174, who remarks that the thirst seems excited by the neighbourhood of a child at the breast).

Several figures are certainly, or possibly, derived from other paintings. As was first pointed out by *de Ricci* ([3] 166) and agreed by *Friedländer* ([9] 106; [40] 59), fig. 1 is a repetition of S. Mary Magdalene in a *Lamentation* by the School of Rogier van der Weyden (see F. *Comparative Material*, p. 17). *Conway* ([3] 163) assumed the terrier in the l. foreground to be based on that in the *Arnolfini Portrait* (M. Davies, *The National Gallery. London (Les Primitifs flamands*, I. *Corpus de la peinture des anciens Pays-Bas méridionaux au quinzième siècle*, 3), II, Antwerp, 1954, No. 47). *Glück* ([19] 56, note 3) claimed more convincingly that it and the dog on the r. are taken from Rogier van der Weyden; they indeed resemble those in the *Columba altarpiece* at Munich possibly of about 1458-59 and in the Antwerp *Sacraments* (E. Panofsky, *Early Netherlandish Painting. Its Origins and Character*, Cambridge, Mass., 1953, II, figs. 352/3 and 347/9). *Friedländer* ([9] 106; [40] 59) refers to the dogs (terrier and greyhound) as a kind of signature of the Master of the Legend of S. Catherine, here introduced, and suggests ([9] 108-109; [40] 60) that they stem from drawings by Rogier van der Weyden; see further, p. 18.
De Ricci connected a number of the heads of the multitude with 15th century portraits, but only one identification has received further support from the critics. He connected fig. 10 with the portrait of a lady then in a Rothschild collection, later reasonably claimed to be Isabella of Portugal (see F. *Comparative Material*). Fig. 7 has certain resemblances to a drawing in the *Mémoriaux* of Antoine de Succa (Brussels, Bibliothèque Royale, Ms. II. 1862, f° 11; Pl. XLVI) of Michelle of France (in reverse; see F. *Comparative Material*). Fig. 11 was unconvincingly claimed by *Bauch* as Jacoba of Bavaria ([33] note 24). Figs. 12 and 13 resemble drawings in the *Mémoriaux* of Succa of John IV and Philip of Saint Pol, Dukes of Brabant (see Pl. XLVI and F. *Comparative Material*). For a possible occurrence of portraits in a painting of this subject, see the panel from the Oratorio of Queen Isabella associated with Juan de Flandes (Madrid, Palacio Real), about 1500, where portraits of King Ferdinand and Queen Isabella of Spain seem to be included among the multitude (*Post, op. cit.*, IV, part 1, 1933, p. 40). This has, however, been doubted by *Elisa Bermejo* (*Juan de Flandes*, Madrid, 1962, p. 13, pl. 1).

The large number of animals distributed in the central panel is unusual, though comparison may be made with *S. Christopher* by the Frankfurt Master (M. J. Friedländer, *Early Netherlandish Painting*, VII. *Quentin Massys*, 1971, pl. 114). Most of the animals are readily identifiable and only those that call for special comment will be discussed here. *Conway* ([3] 163-164) remembered no other such fly as the one on the dress of fig. 1 earlier than the times of Joos van Cleve (active 1511, died 1540/1). Several earlier examples are however noted by *A. Pigler* (*La Mouche peinte: un talisman*, in *Bulletin du Musée hongrois des Beaux-Arts* (Budapest), No. 24, 1964, p. 47-64), of which the fly on the headdress of the woman in the *Double Portrait* of the Frankfurt Master dated 1496 is probably most nearly related in date to the painting here (*Friedländer, op. cit.*, VII, 1971, pl. 117). An ape, placed among an eating and drinking throng in a South German *Marriage at Cana* of c. 1490 has suggested the vice of gluttony (H. W. Janson, *Apes and Ape Lore in the Middle Ages and the Renaissance*, London, 1952, p. 160, note 22, pl. XXI a); here the ape appears to be the pet of fig. 16 without further significance (*ibid.*, p. 150 and 159, note 18, the ape as pet). The owl, which is attacked by swallows among the rocks on the right, occurs in the *Bestiaries* as a symbol of the Jewish people, but such interpretation seems not to make sense here (*Janson, op. cit.*, p. 178 and 196, note 91). The dark bird attacking a white bird on the rock to the right was described by *de Ricci* as an eagle attacking a swan, which he held to be a reference to the house of Hapsburg ([3] 171, note 20). However, the birds appear to be a peregrine falcon and a white egret (the identification of the birds was kindly supplied by *A. R. McEvey*, Curator of Birds, Natural History Museum, Melbourne, report 1965). A mounted camel appears in the upper centre, behind trees.

The following plants occur in the foreground from left to right (Pl. II): A. knapweed (?), B. buttercup (?, the flowers are white with yellow centre), C. great plantain, D. lady's smock; in front of the right hand basket E. an unidentified plant; F. dandelion, G. an unidentified flower (with white butterfly); H. the plant to the right of the ape possibly germander speedwell (the flowers are whitish). On the left behind fig. 1, I. an unidentified plant, which recurs in the r. wing reverse, *S. Peter*, at the height of his knees. The comments on the plants were kindly supplied by Mr. *A. Lawalrée*, Chef de Département of the State Botanical Gardens, Brussels, in a letter of 26.II.1965.

Left wing, obverse
The Marriage at Cana is recorded in the Gospel of *John* (II, 1-11). The scene takes place in a hall into which we look through an arch. An L-shaped table is set. On one side of it are seated nine people in rich dress. At the short arm of the table, under a canopy, the bride between an older and a young woman. The bride wears the traditional crown (*L. Réau, Iconographie de l'art chrétien*, II. 2, *Nouveau Testament*, Paris, 1957, p. 364); her hair is hanging down behind her shoulders as is seen for example in pictures of the same subject accepted as by Bosch and Gerard David (*L. von Baldass, Hieronymus Bosch*, Vienna, 1943, pl. 100; *Adhémar* [34] No. 90). The remaining people at the table are here referred to by the numbers seen in Pl. XII b. No. 5 is holding a beaker with water, No. 6 holds a thin brown slice (? bread).
On the left a standing group, not in fashionable dress; Christ, bearded, has a halo of rays forming a cross; the Virgin in white kerchief and blue mantle, has a round halo. The apostle to the extreme l. is S. Peter, recognizable by his round head, short curly beard and tonsure (*L. Réau, op. cit.*, III, *Iconographie des Saints*, Part III, Paris, 1959, p. 1083); he holds a book. Among the other apostles shown here must be (as is deduced from *John* I, 40, 43, 45) SS. Andrew, Philip and Nathanael (Bartholomew). Another apostle is referred to in *John* (I, 40) without a name, and is traditionally supposed to be S. John himself; he may be the very young apostle here, half hidden behind the heads of Christ and the Virgin (*Réau, op. cit.*, III, Part II, 1958, p. 711). The sixth apostle here is identifiable from tradition as S. James. In front of them six stoneware urns standing on the ground; one of them is being filled with water by a servant. There is some lettering on the hem of his garment (see under D. 3, *Inscriptions*). In the foreground three fashionably clad figures; in the centre, receiving the wine in his cup from the man on the left, is the 'governor' or 'ruler of the feast'; a jewel forming the letter A decorates his cap. The man on the right, whose purse bears the initials *I. M.* is the bridegroom, who was called by the ruler of the feast when he tasted the wine (*John* II, 9). Behind him on the r. a small dog, gnawing a bone.
At the back to the l. we look into a courtyard with a well; a servant is carrying pails of water into the house. A man with a staff looks into the hall through a hatch; above is a polished metal plate under which a candlestick is fastened to the wall. To the r. a man standing next to a sideboard, on which are three jugs and empty bowls. A window with open shutters gives out on to a landscape.

On the consoles of the arch to the l. Samson and the Lion (*Judges* XIV, 5-6). To the r. Gideon's fleece; in *Judges* (VI, 36-40) Gideon addresses the Lord, but he is elsewhere as here shown with an angel *e.g.* in a woodcut in a *Biblia Pauperum* reproduced by *E. Mâle, L'Art religieux de la fin du moyen âge en France. Étude sur l'iconographie du moyen âge et sur ses sources d'inspiration*, Paris, 1922, p. 238, fig. 124. At the top of the arch a medallion with David killing Goliath (I *Samuel*, XVII, 51). Above two niches with statues. To the l. the serpent of the Garden of Eden wound around a tree; it has a bearded male head and pointed ears. To the r. Adam and Eve after the Fall (*Gen.* III, 1-8); the angel usual in representations of this scene is missing. On the roof to the r. of this a peacock displays its tail.

The main features of the picture correspond to the text in *John* (II, 1-11). The guests are there not explicitly referred to, but are implied.

Christ and the Virgin here do not sit at table with the guests but together with the six apostles form a group standing apart. In Flemish paintings of this subject such as those by Bosch and David (referred to above) Christ and the Virgin occupy places at the table and the apostles are missing, except apparently S. John, who in accordance with a traditional identification of him as the bridegroom is recognizable sitting to the l. of the bride in Bosch's picture.

A composition similar to the picture here is to be found in the Retable of the *Transfiguration* assigned to the School of the Master of S. George (*Ch. R. Post, A History of Spanish Painting*, Cambridge, Mass., II, 1930, p. 420 seq., fig. 234). In that picture the table has a comparable shape; Christ accompanied by the Virgin and four apostles stands to the left performing the miracle. In the altarpiece of 1499 in San Lorenzo della Costa commissioned by Andrea della Costa, by an unknown Bruges master, Christ and the Virgin without apostles stand in the foreground on the r.; the foreshortened table with the guests is on the l. (*A. Morassi, Trittico fiammingo a San Lorenzo della Costa*, Florence, 1947). A similarly shaped table occurs in Jerome Bosch's picture referred to above; the sideboard and the servant on the r. in this picture may also be compared.

Various relics of urns held to have been used at the Marriage at Cana are known (see *F. de Mély, Vases de Cana*, in *Fondation Eugène Piot. Monuments et Mémoires* (Paris), Vol. X, 1903, p. 145-170, and *F. Cabrol* and *H. Leclerc, Dictionnaire d'archéologie chrétienne et de liturgie*, Vol. II, 2, Paris, 1925, cols. 1818-19). *Smits* refers to Molanus, who says that the urn at Cologne was the source for various representations of the miracle (*Smits* [16] 74); this claim has been made for the urns occurring in several Flemish paintings of the period, such as those already referred to by David and Bosch, and some others (see *Adhémar* [34] 116). The Melbourne urns however resemble most closely the Bamberg urn reproduced by *Mély* (*op. cit.*, p. 158, fig. 7).

The sharp foreshortening of one end of the table may have been adopted here to suit the format of the wing. Long tables set at right angles to the picture plane are quite frequently found in 15th century manuscript illuminations, particularly in the representations of secular banquets. An illumination by Philippe de Mazerolles in the *Histoire du Bon Roi Alexandre*, executed for Philip the Good, shows such a table with a sideboard at the back (*P. Durrieu, La Miniature flamande au temps de la Cour de Bourgogne (1415-1530)*, Paris/Brussels, 1927, 68-69, pl. XLIV, Musée Dutuit, Petit Palais, Paris, Ms. 456, fol. 88).

Since *Seymour de Ricci*'s article ([3] 164 seq.) it has been generally accepted that many of the figures in this panel are portraits of members of the House of Burgundy. The only figures identifiable with certainty by their resemblance to existing portraits are 1. Philip the Good; 6. Philip the Fair of Austria; 8. Adolph of Cleves; 7., less certainly, resembles Engelbert II of Nassau. The features seen in a number of different portraits seem to suggest that 5. is Maximilian I of Austria. From his position it would appear that 3. is Charles the Bold; the general shape of his head accords with known portraits. On the assumption that the wives are seated to the r. of their husbands it has sometimes been held that the three women at the short arm of the table are the three wives of Philip the Good (*Friedländer* [17] 18; *Onghena* [30] 111); they do however not resemble any known portrait of Michelle of France and Bonne of Artois and Isabella of Portugal. On the same assumption 2. should be one of the wives of Charles the Bold, 4. the wife of Maximilian; they bear indeed some resemblance to portraits of Margaret of York and of Mary of Burgundy. Philip the Fair appears unmarried. For related portraits see F. *Comparative Material*. Some alterations and adjustments to the prototypes have been made; in particular, the insignia of the Golden Fleece, which are nowhere shown in this picture, have been altered to generalized ornaments.

The presence of Old Testament scenes in the arch above raises the question whether these may have typological significance. In the *Biblia Pauperum* the scenes occurring here of Samson and the Lion and David and Goliath prefigure the Descent into Hell (*e.g. J. J. M. Timmers, Symboliek en Iconographie der Christelijke Kunst*, Roermond/ Maaseik, 1947, § 623). Gideon's fleece and Eve and the Serpent prefigure the Annunciation (*E. Mâle, op. cit.*, p. 238, fig. 124). The peacock carries symbolic meanings of Immortality, the Resurrection and other things, as recorded by *L. Charbonneau-Lassay, Le Bestiaire du Christ*, (Bruges, 1940), p. 617 *seq.*; but such meanings do not seem to make sense here. For the eucharistic significance of the Marriage at Cana, see p. 10.

Right wing, obverse
In the r. foreground Lazarus stands upright in a grave, the stone of which lies displaced. On the stone, marks suggestive of lettering and perhaps of the words *Lazare veni foras* (see below). A man takes the winding sheet off his raised arms, which suggest a gesture of prayer. Lazarus looks up at Christ (Pl. XX b, fig. 1), Who wears a tunic, is bearded and has a halo of rays in the form of a cross. On Christ's l. S. Peter (fig. 2) with round head, short curly beard and tonsure (*L. Réau, Iconographie de l'Art chrétien*, III, *Iconographie des Saints*, Part III, Paris, 1959, p. 1083). Further to the r. Martha (?) (fig. 3), in dress of the painter's time; to the r. again, S. John (?) (fig. 4), youthful and without a beard (*Réau, op. cit.*, III, Part II, 1958, p. 711). Other figures are in garments of the painter's time; to the l. behind Christ one (fig. 5) holds a cloth to his nose. Close to Lazarus in the foreground, and kneeling, Mary (?), putting her hand with a transparent veil between her face and the grave. The two women and Christ are shown weeping. In the sky the half figure of God, bareheaded in an aureole of clouds; Christ looks up at Him. In the l. background a castle built over water, which extends towards the distance. To the r. a gate of a city or perhaps of a castle, on a rocky hill. Below this, small figures of Christ with SS. Peter and John and two other apostles; a woman (Mary or Martha), kneels before Him and there are some bystanders. Another woman (Martha or Mary) is further back. In the foreground, below Lazarus, A. meadow buttercup; in the lower r. hand corner, B. probably campion; to the r. of Lazarus, C. woodruff (the plants were identified by Mr. *A. Lawalrée*).
The raising of Lazarus is recorded in the Gospel of *S. John* (XI, 1-44); it does not occur in the other gospels. The main features of the picture correspond with the text. The iconographical history of the theme is given in *E. Mâle, La Résurrection de Lazare dans l'Art*, in *La Revue des Arts* (Paris), Vol. 1, 1951, p. 44-52, and in *H. Aurenhammer, Lexikon der Christlichen Ikonographie*, Part 3, Vienna, 1961, *Auferweckung des Lazarus*, p. 249 *seq.* Here only some points will receive comment that are unusual in the depiction of this theme in Northern Europe in or about the 15th century.

In several 15th century pictures Lazarus appears seated in the grave (so Geertgen tot Sint Jans, *E. Panofsky, Early Netherlandish Painting, op. cit.*, 1953, II, fig. 442) or seated on the tombstone (as in Albert van Ouwater, *Panofsky, op. cit.*, fig. 435) or kneeling on the tombstone (as in a painting by the Bruges Master in the *Costa Triptych*, already referred to under *Marriage at Cana*). Here Lazarus is standing in the grave. In a woodcut of 1486, Lazarus is shown thus, from the back (*J. E. Snyder, The Early Haarlem School of Painting*, in *The Art Bulletin*, Vol. XLII, 1960, p. 53, fig. 21). In a Dutch Book of Hours at The Hague, Lazarus is depicted walking in his grave, held by the hands by S. Peter, who kneels before him on the ground (*A. W. Byvanck* and *G. J. Hoogewerff, Noord-Nederlandsche Miniaturen*, The Hague, I, 1922, pl. 35). Lazarus appears to be standing or walking in a picture associated with Juan de Flandes (*E. Bermejo, Juan de Flandes*, Madrid, 1962, pl. 5).

The untying of the hands of Lazarus seems to be peculiar to representations of this theme in Northern style of the latter part of the 15th century; it is to be found for example in Nicolas Froment's Uffizi *Triptych* of 1461 (*Mâle, op. cit.*, fig. 5). A phrase in *Matthew* (XVI, 19) may have suggested the view that the loosing was by S. Peter (see further *Mâle, op. cit.*, p. 49-51); the text of *John* does not specify him, suggesting rather that a member of the crowd performed the untying, and this is what is shown here.

The representation of a second theme from the same gospel text in the background is rare for this subject in early Netherlandish art. Such a scene is to be found in the *Raising of Lazarus* accepted as by Geertgen tot Sint Jans, in the Louvre, Paris, where two women (Mary and Martha) kneel before Christ accompanied by S. Peter and two other figures, presumably apostles (*Panofsky, op. cit.*, II, fig. 442). The scene shown in the Melbourne picture would seem to illustrate *John* (XI, 32).

There is some pseudo-lettering on the gravestone but inscriptions are quite frequent in representations of this theme. Froment's picture (see above) has "*Lazare veni foras*" from *John* (XI, 43). In Juan de Flandes' picture, apparently just *Lasara* (*Bermejo, op. cit.*, pl. 5). For inscriptions in works of Jean Bourdichon and Jan Joest, see *Mâle, op. cit.*, figs. 6, 7.

The *Raising of Lazarus* is represented as a symbol of the resurrection of all men in the early period in the murals in the catacombs and on early Christian sarcophagi (*F. Cabrol* and *H. Leclerc, op. cit.*, Vol. VIII, 2, cols. 2011 ff.). This becomes rare in art in the Middle Ages, but is maintained in the liturgy in the Mass of the Dead.

Panofsky sees a reference to the resurrection at the Last Judgment in the picture of the *Raising of Lazarus* by Ouwater (*op. cit.*, Vol. I, p. 320-1). Such meaning is clearly alluded to in a woodcut from the lower Rhine of c. 1480, where the *Raising of Lazarus* is accompanied by an inscription: "*Ego sum resurrectio et vita qui credit in me: etiam si mortuus fuerit vivet*" (*W. L. Schreiber, Handbuch der Holz- und Metallschnitte des XV. Jahrhunderts*, Leipzig, I, 1926, p. 51, No. 145). The first five words of this inscription occur on the frame of a shutter of the picture by Froment (see *G. Ring, A Century of French Painting, 1400-1500*, London, 1949, pl. 119).

Mme *Veronee* (letter March 15, 1965) pointed out that in *John* (VI, 54) Christ subsequent to the miracle of the loaves and fishes promises that the Eucharist will bestow eternal life on the receiver. If an eucharistic meaning is assumed for the *Multiplication of the Loaves and Fishes* and the *Marriage at Cana* here, the *Raising of Lazarus* considered as a symbol of the resurrection could stand meaningfully alongside them.

Left wing, reverse

The Virgin, seated on a grassy bench, offers an apple to the Child, who sits upright on her r. knee; to the l. a dragon tree with two lizards on its trunk; in the l. middle distance the ass, a stag and a date palm with five angels bending it towards S. Joseph on the r. In the distance a walled town. Above, in a break in the clouds,

God is blessing; He is wearing a tiara encircled by one crown and surmounted by a cross; three rays descend from Him towards the Holy Ghost as a dove. In the foreground, from l. to r. a lizard; knapweed (but of a different species from the one in the *Multiplication of the Loaves and Fishes*); spiked speedwell; and an unidentified plant, which recurs in the central panel (Pl. II). (The comments on the plants and trees were kindly supplied by Mr. *A. Lawalrée*, Chef de Département of the State Botanical Gardens, Brussels, in a letter of 26.II.1965). *Matthew* (II, 13-14) records the *Flight into Egypt*. Here it is a *Repose on the Flight*. Various legends of the *Flight* and the *Repose* are recorded in *Pseudo-Matthew*. In ch. XX it is there recorded that on the third day of the journey the Virgin, sitting down under a palm tree, longed for its fruit; Jesus, sitting in Mary's lap, bade the tree bend down, which it did, to her feet and she gathered the dates. An angel in connection with a branch of the tree is mentioned in the continuation of this story in *Pseudo-Matthew*, ch. XXI.

Angels and a bending palm tree may be seen in a *Flight to Egypt* assigned to the Maestro delle Vele, S. Francesco, Assisi, of the first half of the 14th century (*R. van Marle, The Development of the Italian Schools of Painting*, The Hague, III, 1924, fig. 126). An early representation of a *Repose* with a bending tree and the Virgin gathering the fruit appears in a Book of Hours, in the Walters Art Gallery, Baltimore (W. 211 E, dated by Miss Dorothy Miner c. 1420; repr. *E. Panofsky, Early Netherlandish Painting, op. cit.*, 1953, II, fig. 191).
Martin Schongauer, in the engraving of the *Flight to Egypt* (B 7; *M. Lehrs, Martin Schongauer*, Berlin, 1914, pl. VI and the same, [8] 62-64, No. 7) may well have invented the motif of the angels bending the tree, as is claimed by *Vogler* ([14] 35, 65).
Parts of Schongauer's engraving (dated in the early seventies by *J. Baum, Martin Schongauer*, Vienna, 1948, p. 37) have served as models for the painting here. Not only the motif but the form of the palm tree with angels, the dragon tree with a parrot in its branches, two lizards on its trunk, another lizard on the ground below, the trees described as fig trees by *Lehrs* ([8] 15), the spiked speedwell in the foreground and the figure of Joseph and the ass are borrowed from the engraving with a change of prominence in certain cases; the ass (in the background in the picture) is inverted from the engraving. Several other paintings deriving from Schongauer's engraving are listed by *Lehrs* ([8] 64). The motif of angels bending the palm tree became fairly popular; it is used by Correggio, in *La Zingarella*, Naples, Museo e Gallerie Nazionali di Capodimonte (repr. *Corrado Ricci, Correggio*, London/New York, 1930, pl. XXXVI) and in *The Madonna of the Bowl*, Parma Art Gallery (*ibid.*, pl. CLXIV, 96 ff.).

The poses of the Madonna and Child, with the Child holding an apple, are somewhat related to various pictures assigned to the Master of the Magdalen Legend such as *Friedländer* [17] pl. VI; *E. Michel, Musée national du Louvre, Catalogue raisonné des Peintures du Moyen Age, de la Renaissance et des Temps Modernes. Peintures flamandes du XVe et du XVIe siècle*, Paris, 1953, fig. 104; *Corpus Leningrad* (1965, No. 112, 62). The Child's pose is similar to that in a Rogieresque *Virgin and Child with Four Saints*, Cook Collection sale, Christie's, 25th November, 1966, lot 58 repr., where the Child also holds an apple. The apple may refer to the Redemption from the Fall (see *J. J. M. Timmers, Symboliek en Iconographie der Christelijke Kunst*, Roermond/Maaseik, 1947, § 1908). The dragon tree and the parrot, the fig trees and the palm tree introduce southern local colour (for the dragon tree, see *H. Schenck, Martin Schongauers Drachenbaum*, 1920, offprint from *Naturwissenschaftliche Wochenschrift*, Jena, No. 49, 5 December 1920, p. 775-780, *Lehrs* [8] 15-16, and *G. Pochat, Der Exotismus während des Mittelalters und der Renaissance, Acta Universitatis Stockholmiensis, Stockholm Studies in History of Art*, 21, Uppsala, 1970, p. 118-124).

Right wing, reverse

S. Peter in three-quarter profile, facing left, holding two keys in his right hand and a book in his left, stands in a landscape among hills and trees. In the foreground from left to right the following plants (Pl. XXX-XXXI and XXXIII):

A. *Iris germanica*, german iris;

B. an unidentified plant which occurs again in the *Martyrdom of SS. Crispin and Crispinian*, Warsaw, National Gallery (*Białostocki* [36] No. 113, p. 5, u);

C. probably *Chelidonium majus*, greater celandine, though the petals are rather white than yellow;

D. *Veronica chamedrys L*, germander speedwell;

E. probably *Viola odorata*, sweet violet;

F. *Plantago major*, great plantain;

G. *Chrysanthemum leucanthemum L.*, marguerite;

H. *Ranunculus acris*, meadow buttercup.

Level with S. Peter's keys, at left (Pl. XXIX): three unidentified plants; just below them (Pl. XXIV b and XXIX): stylized *Sarothamnus scoparius L.* (*Wimmer*), broom which recurs at Warsaw (No. 113, p. 5, a).

To the right of S. Peter, abreast of his knee (Pl. XXIV b): an unidentified plant which recurs in central panel, I (Pl. II and III) and at Warsaw (No. 113, p. 5, x).

(Identification of the plants by Mr. *A. Lawalrée*).

The representation of S. Peter follows the traditional western iconography; he has a tonsure and tufts of hair over the forehead, a short beard and bare hands and feet. He often holds two keys (to 'bind' and to 'loose', *Matthew* (XVI, 19); *L. Réau, Iconographie de l'art chrétien*, III, *Iconographie des Saints*, Part III, Paris, 1959, p. 1083).

It would be difficult to find a common theme for all five painted surfaces; the following comments refer particularly to the panels of the interior. The combination of the *Multiplication of the Loaves and Fishes* on the central panel with the *Marriage at Cana* on the left wing and perhaps also the repeated emphasis on drinking in the former raise the question whether an eucharistic significance was intended here (*Aurenhammer* [35] 417). These two subjects are in early times standard subjects for indicating the Eucharist (see *F. Cabrol* and *H. Leclerc*, *Dictionnaire d'archéologie chrétienne et de liturgie*, Vol. II, 2, Paris, 1925, cols. 1802-19 and Vol. XIII, 1, 1937, cols. 436-458). Both themes still appear in medieval typology as prototypes of the *Last Supper*, but they are represented less frequently after the 13th century and an eucharistic significance often cannot be clearly established. The two subjects are shown on the same page with presumed eucharistic significance in the *Très Belles Heures de Notre-Dame* associated with Jacquemart de Hesdin, dated by *Panofsky* c. 1385-1390 (*Early Netherlandish Painting*, *op. cit.*, p. 45; *P. Durrieu, Les Très Belles Heures de Notre-Dame du Duc Jean de Berry*, Paris, 1922, p. 49-50, pl. VIII; this was pointed out by Dr. *Rosalie B. Green*, Index of Christian Art, Princeton University, in a letter to *Martin Davies*, 10.II.1965).

In the already mentioned *S. Wolfgang altarpiece* of 1471-81 by Michael Pacher the *Marriage at Cana* and the *Multiplication of the Loaves and Fishes* are placed side by side; this has suggested an eucharistic implication (*E. Hempel, Das Werk Michael Pachers*, Vienna, 1940, p. 22, pl. 66, and *Schiller* [37] Vol. I, p. 175).

Mme *Veronee-Verhaegen* has drawn our attention to the painted wings of what was probably a sculptured altarpiece from the studio of Colyn de Coter, recorded in the collection of Mme Heinemann, Wiesbaden. The outside of these wings show the *Baptism*, the *Multiplication of the Loaves and Fishes*, *Abraham and Melchisedek* and the *Marriage at Cana* (see *J. Maquet-Tombu, Colijn de Coter, peintre bruxellois*, Brussels, 1937, p. 87-88, pl. XXXV, and letter from *N. Veronee-Verhaegen*, Brussels, 31.VIII.1965). Since the scene of *Abraham and Melchisedek* is a well known typological equivalent of the *Last Supper*, as for instance in the *Holy Sacrament altar* at Louvain by Dieric Bouts of 1468, the association of this theme with the *Marriage at Cana* and the *Multiplication of the Loaves and Fishes* by de Coter suggests that an eucharistic significance could have been intended there. While the eucharistic significance of the Multiplication and the Marriage at Cana is rarely to be established in the later Middle Ages some examples will be quoted to show that the tradition was dormant rather than dead, and was readily re-awakened in the 16th and 17th centuries.

For further reference to types of the Eucharist see *L. Richeome, Tableaux Sacrez des figures mystiques du Très-Auguste Sacrifice et Sacrement de l'Eucharistie*, Paris, 1601, *Multiplication* on p. 349 *seq.* and *B. Knipping, De Iconografie van de Contra-Reformatie in de Nederlanden*, Hilversum, I, 1939, p. 246-247.

The *Multiplication of the Loaves and Fishes* and some other eucharistic themes are shown in proximity to the *Last Supper* in Tintoretto's ceiling and wall paintings at one end of the upper hall of the Scuola di San Rocco at Venice (1576-81) (*E. Newton, Tintoretto*, London, 1952, p. 126-127); and one may wonder if there was here an eucharistic intention.

Later, three clear cases of eucharistic significance are found :

1. in Cavaliere Cesari d'Arpino's decoration of the choir vault of the Certosa of S. Martino at Naples, of 1589-91. The description in *B. de Dominici, Vite de' Pittori, Scultori, ed Architetti Napolitani*, Naples, II, 1743, p. 263, gives the four main fields of the vault as the *Gathering of Manna, Elijah and the Angel*, the *Multiplication of the Loaves and Fishes*, and the *Last Supper*, adding: "Tutte figure della Sacra Eucaristia". The four subsidiary areas are the *Marriage at Cana*, the *Feast of Simon, Ahimelech offering the Shewbread to David*, the *Supper at Emmaus*, but are not so commented on by *Dominici*.

2. in Lanfranco's decoration from the early 1620's of the chapel of the SS. Sacramento in S. Paolo fuori le Mura at Rome. These include large pictures of the *Last Supper* and the *Multiplication of the Loaves and Fishes*, now at Dublin (Cat. 1963?, p. 74), and a number of Old Testament types of the Eucharist. The seventeenth century writers Bellori and Passeri both begin their description stressing that the whole scheme concerns the Eucharist (for this decoration, see *B. L. La Penta*, in the *Bollettino d'Arte* (Rome), Jan.-June 1963, p. 54 ff. and *E. Schleier, Lanfrancos Malereien der Sacramentskapelle in S. Paolo fuori le Mura in Rom*, in *Arte Antica e Moderna* (Bologna), 1965, (part I) No. 29, p. 62 ff.; (part II) No. 30, p. 188 ff.; (part III) Nos. 31-32, p. 343 ff.).

3. in the grisailles of S. Bavo at Ghent by P. N. van Reysschoot (1789-91) one subject is the *Multiplication of the Loaves and Fishes* and several of the subjects are clearly eucharistic (see complete list in *E. Dhanens, Inventaris van het Kunstpatrimonium van Oostvlaanderen*, V, *Sint-Baafskathedraal. Gent*, Ghent, 1965, p. 219-221).

Triptychs uniquely representing miracles seem most unusual. The following works might be cited as comparable, but only the first of these is a close parallel.

1. Triptych, in the Almshouse, Sherborne, in the Flemish taste, claimed to be probably School of Cologne, last quarter 15th century; this shows the *Raising of Lazarus* in the central panel. Each wing (inside) contains a miracle as main subject with another miracle in the background, so that five miracles are depicted in all (*Royal Commission on Historical Monuments, England, An Inventory of the Historical Monuments in Dorset*, Vol. I, *West*, London, 1952, p. 212; included in *Exhibition of British Primitive Paintings, Royal Academy of Arts*, London, 1923, Cat. (Oxford), 1924, p. 29 f., No. 47; cf. *M. Conway, British Primitives*, in *The Burlington Magazine* (London), Vol. XLIII, 1923, p. 223 B, repr.

2. Nicolas Froment, triptych, dated 1461, where the *Resurrection of Lazarus* together with the related episodes of *Martha announcing the death of Lazarus to Christ* and *Mary Magdalene annointing Christ's Feet* are depicted on the three inner panels (G. Ring, *A Century of French Painting, 1400-1500*, London, 1949, Cat. No. 214, figs. 118-120).

3. The altarpiece in San Lorenzo della Costa near Genoa, by a Bruges Master of 1499, containing in the l. wing obverse the *Miracle at Cana* and in the r. wing obverse the *Raising of Lazarus* (A. Morassi, *Trittico fiammingo a San Lorenzo della Costa*, Florence, 1947). *F. Cabrol* and *H. Leclerc* (*op. cit.*, II, 2, col. 1813) refer to these miracles as first and last in the public life of Christ.

4. The wings of a retable in Brussels, Musées Royaux des Beaux-Arts, Nos. 110 a, b, signed by Jan van Coninxloo, which show the *Marriage at Cana, Christ in the Temple* and on the other side, distributed over both wings, the *Miracle of the Loaves and Fishes* (Rep. ACL Nos. 6019 C, 117.460 B and 117.461 B).

5. A triptych of the School of Leyden in the Schlossmuseum at Krefeld, where the *Miracle of the Loaves and Fishes* extends over all three panels (G. J. Hoogewerff, *De Noord-Nederlandsche Schilderkunst*, The Hague, Vol. III, 1939, fig. 203).

The shape of the altarpiece is hardly to be met with before 1500 in the Netherlands. True, the top of the central panel resembles in shape that of the *Double Portrait* assigned to the Master of Frankfurt, dated 1496 (*M. J. Friedländer, Early Netherlandish Painting, op. cit.*, VII, 1971, pl. 117; Mme *Veronee-Verhaegen* kindly drew our attention to this picture). A picture with a top to some extent of comparable shape assigned to Albert Bouts, the *Annunciation* in Berlin, is dated by *Friedländer* c. 1495 but is unfortunately perhaps cut (*M. J. Friedländer, op. cit.*, III, *Dieric Bouts and Joos van Gent*, 1968, pl. 60, No. 44 b). An altarpiece to cite is Albert Bouts' *Assumption of the Virgin*, Brussels Museum, dated by *Schöne* about 1500 (*W. Schöne, Dieric Bouts und seine Schule*, Berlin/Leipzig, 1938, p. 204-5; *M. J. Friedländer, op. cit.*, III, pl. 70-71); Bosch's *Adoration of the Magi*, Madrid, is dated by *Baldass* after 1500 (*L. von Baldass, Hieronymus Bosch*, Vienna, 1943, p. 248, fig. 93). While the portrait by the Frankfurt Master supports the idea that the triptych could have been painted shortly before 1500, the shape is certainly more usual some years later, when it became for a time very common. Admittedly the style of the Melbourne picture is rather noticeably out of date for post-1500.

2. *Colours*

Central panel, The Multiplication of the Loaves and Fishes

The general impression is multicoloured, vivid but not brilliant. The landscape setting is a yellowish green, the rocks on the left and elsewhere being yellow-brown on top. The lake in the distance is light blue, the city light brown with pale red and blue roofs. To the right and left of the city, blue-green hills. Light blue mountains in the far distance. The sky is dark blue at the top gradually lightening to a pinkish white on the horizon. The figures stand in vivid colouring against the light toned landscape. The numbering of the figures refers to Pl. II. 1. White headdress, white cloak shaded with blue and lined with olive green; crimson robe. 2. Dressed entirely in black; cloak edged with brown fur. 3. Hennin embroidered with red and white dots; brown robe edged with fur at sleeves; a blue placard, white belt and grey and white fur or drapings over the bodice. 4. Dark grey cap, yellow garment shaded with red; grey beard. 5. Blue-white hat, olive green cloak, blue stockings. 6. Light brown hair; scarlet robe lined with grey fur at the hem; blue-white mantle. 7. White hood, small white collar inside brown fur collar; black placard. 8. White hood; crimson robe with grey fur collar; dark grey mantle. 9. Brownish-white beard, grey-black cap; the cloak a slightly lighter grey. 10. Semi-translucent veil over yellow-brown coif; blue robe, with crimson collar; white belt and white placard. 11. Brown cauls under white hood; crimson robe lined with white fur. 12. Dark green headdress, grey cloak patterned with a lighter grey, lined with brown fur at the neck. 13. Dark-brown hair, black cloak, edged with brown fur at neck and sleeves. The small girl in front of fig. 13: blue-black headdress over light-brown hair; brown robe patterned with blue and lined with white. The little boy next to the girl: light-brown hair, blue robe. 14. Brown cauls, white veil; green robe lined with grey fur and similar cuffs, a red underskirt lined with white fur. 15. Blue-white headdress, blue-black robe edged at sleeves and hem with brown fur; red cloak; whitish blue stockings. 16. Blue hat with red brim; a golden (yellow) and green brocade jacket, long dark-blue sleeves and underskirt; jacket and skirt edged with gold. The chain of the sword is golden yellow, its hilt golden yellow and dark grey; its sheath red. The apostle in front: dark blue robe lined with yellow; hair brown. The apostle behind him: crimson robe, white coat; hair light brown. Similar colours to the ones described appear among the figures in the back rows. Some exceptions will be noted. In the row leading from fig. 7 to the left the fourth figure from the edge has a light blue robe shaded with crimson. Similar colours appear in the robe of the young beardless apostle further to the left holding a basket in front of a seated figure in a white robe, shaded in pink. The group of Christ and the Apostles in the middle distance: Christ wears a grey-blue robe, his hair and beard are brown. Apostles to the left of Christ: white robe, hair reddish-brown; blue robe, hair brown. Behind, to the left of Christ: light brown robe, hair light grey; to the right of Christ: scarlet robe, hair grey; grey robe and dark brown hair; crimson robe, brown hair. The little boy is in olive green; hair reddish-blonde. Figures at the well: the woman in white headdress and blue-white robe; the man in scarlet, knees bare, dark grey stockings; sword grey and black with golden yellow ornaments. God the Father appears surrounded by dark blue clouds in a yellow aureole; He wears a red robe and white tiara; angels shaded-in in red. The flasks are grey, the baskets of bread light brown. Two dogs in the foreground are white, the monkey and the dog on the extreme right are brown.

Left wing obverse, Marriage at Cana
The total impression is multicoloured but not brilliant. The arch is brownish-grey; the walls greyish-buff. The tiles of the floor are buff, green, light brown and light blue; the window shutters brown, the landscape yellow, brown and green, Christ wears a dark violet-brown robe, slightly lighter than that of fig. 7; his hair and beard are light brown. S. Peter in scarlet robe, with brown belt. His cloak is dark green, his hair light grey. The Virgin has a white headdress and blue robe. Between S. Peter and Christ an apostle in light blue, with light brown hair; above S. Peter's head an apostle in pink with brown hair. To the left of him brown hair, white hair, light brown hair. The servant has a scarlet hat with green brim, and a garment striped in various shades of yellow and light brown, violet-brown hose. The jug is dark brown with black bands, the urns light brown. The man carrying water at the back has a pinkish crimson hat, blue jacket over a light brown vest and sleeves. His apron is white, his hose scarlet, the shoes black. He carries light brown pails rimmed with black. The man in the hatch wears a violet-pink hat and similar robe over a white vest and light brown sleeves. The three figures at the short end of the table from l. to r.: white hood, scarlet robe lined with grey, white placard, green belt with golden yellow ornaments. The centre figure in pinkish crimson robe, lined with white at the neckline; white cuffs; a black placard; hair light brown; crown golden yellow with greyish pearls and bright red decoration on top. The next: green-black hood veiled hennin, white robe patterned with grey, edged at neck and sleeves with golden yellow bands.

Figures numbered in Pl. XII b. 1. Black hat and gown, golden yellow jewellery. 2. Black hood, veiled hennin, grey-violet robe with white cuffs and collar, gold brocade placard; golden yellow and orange necklace with greyish pearls. 3. Red hat with ermine brim, rimmed with golden yellow crown with greyish pearls, a golden yellow jewel with grey pearls in front; gold brocade cloak edged at sleeves with brown fur, over a white undergarment; black band around neckline hanging down at left. 4. Black hood, veiled hennin; crimson gown edged with white, laced across a black placard. 5. Red and gold brocade garment, brown fur cloak; yellow golden jewellery; light brown-grey hair. 6. Black hat with yellow golden jewel, red cloak with ermine collar over a black and gold brocade robe; hair light brown. 7. Black hat, dark violet-brown cloak edged with brown at sleeves and neck; brocade robe, black stockings; hair brown. 8. Black hat with golden yellow jewel and greyish white pearl; gold and black brocade cloak, brown fur collar and lining; grey-black robe, red sleeves and inner collar; brown boots with beige cuffs; hair dark grey. 9. Violet-brown hat with golden yellow jewel; crimson cloak with light brown fur collar, flecked with dark brown; black robe; the purse grey-brown black with golden yellow lettering and greyish pearls; shoes brown-black. The baldachin has a violet-brown canopy; yellow golden brocade hanging with black pattern; the columns are blue-black with lighter marbling except the one on the left front which is violet-brown with lighter marbling. The plate above the candlestick is golden yellow, the jugs and bowls on the sideboard are blue black edged with golden yellow. The servant next to it is dressed in black hat and coat, with brown collar and violet-brown vest. On the table, spread with a grey white table-cloth, the breads are light brown; the silverware is grey-blue with golden ornaments; the pieces of meat are brown, the wine reddish purple, the glass is green in the upper part, pink in the lower part.

Right wing obverse, Raising of Lazarus
The total impression is slightly more brilliant than the other panels (Pl. XX). 1. Christ wears a violet-blue garment, hair and beard brown, his eyes, grey-blue. Lazarus' fleshcolour is natural, though face and hands are yellow-greyish, his white graveclothes are shaded with grey. The kneeling female figure in the foreground wears a crimson dress, with neckline and short sleeves decorated with gold design and greyish pearls; long yellow sleeves stippled in light green and dark green; headdress white with transparent veils. The man loosing Lazarus has a yellow hat with dark violet inner brim; his blue coat with brown fur collar is edged with brown fur at arm openings and hem: his fleshtones noticeably shaded with grey. To the left from Christ: 6. A man with black hat. 5. A man with blue-white hat, in a green brocade garment with orange and yellow dotted highlights; a blue-white belt; underneath a crimson frock with blue line near the hem; part of the same frock heavily highlighted with yellow-green, is held to the man's nose; black sandal over brown hose. 7. A man with scarlet brim on dark crimson hat and another with black brown hat. To the right of Christ: 2. S. Peter with grey hair and blue garment. A head with transparent headdress, golden band and grey pearl. 3. The woman with hands across her chest wears a white headdress with golden jewel; her hair is light brown; blue mantle, scarlet brocade dress, underneath which appears a black garment; green belt and dark brown sleeves. 4. S. John in light brown hair and crimson garment. A man in profile, with violet hat on light brown hair, garment striped light blue and pink, with olive green sleeves and a yellow neckline; underneath a white garment; the hose is crimson, the shoes black. The sword has brown and grey hilt and brown sheath. Further back two heads with dark violet-brown hats and light and dark grey garments.
In the background Christ is in blue-grey; the figures behind him to the left are in pink, grey blue and scarlet. The kneeling woman is in red, blue and yellow; the onlookers to the right are in light brown, pink, grey and crimson garments and have crimson, blue and white hats. God the Father is painted in scarlet, against a yellow

aureole, edged with scarlet clouds, and surrounded by dark clouds; the sky is dark blue, shading to white towards the horizon. The landscape in the distance light blue; the architecture grey-buff; the castle on the left has a grey-blue roof; the trees and the ground are a brown-yellow-green, the rocks in the foreground and the lid of the tomb dark grey.

Left wing, reverse, The Repose on the Flight to Egypt
The Virgin has reddish-brown hair, dark grey eyes; her robe is crimson with gold pattern and grey pearls at hem; her dress is blue, the halo gold; the Christ Child sits on a white cloth; the apple is red and greenish brown. S. Joseph wears a violet-brown coat, his hair is grey-brown, he has a white bag and brownish-yellow flask. The ass is grey. The angels in the palm tree from left to right have 1. grey blue dress, crimson-lined cloak, crimson and blue wings, auburn hair; 2. blue dress, crimson and blue wings, fair hair; 3. (underneath stem of palm) yellow dress, fair hair; 4. yellow dress, shaded with red, crimson and yellow wings; 5. blue dress, scarlet cloak, crimson and blue wings, fair hair. God the Father is in a crimson robe, rimmed with gold, crimson tiara and crown; the globe is blue-white with gold band; the aureole is yellow with red rays and some red clouds, surrounded by dark blue clouds; the dove is white, the rays are gold. The landscape is brown-green in foreground, green in middle distance, pale yellow green and blue in far distance. The houses are grey with blue roofs; the city wall is pink, the river light blue. The trees have dark brown trunks, brown green leaves; the lizards are various shades of brown with some yellow.

Right wing, reverse, S. Peter
S. Peter in scarlet robe and crimson cloak; he has dark grey hair and grey-brown eyes. Keys grey, book grey-black, page ends light greenish brown; hands markedly shaded with grey; face ruddy; gold halo. Landscape and plants in foreground a brown-green, dark green trees with lighter dots in middle distance, hills at back blue and yellow, trees light blue with yellow dots. Iris blue and violet with yellow.

3. *Inscriptions and Heraldry*

In the l. wing, *Marriage at Cana*, lettering occurs around the hem of the garment of the servant pouring water into the jugs; it appears to read *AIVERSTEN S* or *RIVERZTEN S;* perhaps it is an evocation of "*Ravenstein*", a title of Adoph of Cleves.
The latter wears on his hat a jewel which is the letter "A", the initial of his Christian name.
On the jug held by Engelbert of Nassau (?), there is an unidentified escutcheon.
On the purse of the bridegroom: *I.M.*. It may be noted that these letters appear to be of merely decorative significance; similar letters *IM* surmounted by a cross, occur three times in the glass of the window of the central panel and l. wing of the triptych of the *Last Supper* assigned to the Catherine Master in the Seminary in Bruges (*Friedländer* [9] 105 and No. 48, pl. XLVI; [40] pl. 51: not visible on the plate; Cat. Exhibition *Dieric Bouts*, Brussels, Delft, 1957/8, No. 77, with comment). For letters probably used as ornament, see *M. Davies, National Gallery Catalogues. Early Netherlandish School*, London, 1955, Gerard David, No. 1079, where *AW* occurs on the purse of the Moorish King. See also *The Sacrifice of Isaac* by the Frankfurt Master of about 1500, where similar lettering occurs on the hem of the servant on the lower right and in the centre (*R. Fritz, Sammlung Becker*, Dortmund, 1967, No. 38, rep.).
In the r. wing, *Raising of Lazarus*, there is only pseudo-lettering on the gravestone.

In the l. wing reverse, *The Repose on the Flight to Egypt*, on the border of the Virgin's robe lettering can be read: *MVA IHEΣO | ...V... MEOTÆ.*

E. ORIGIN AND SUBSEQUENT HISTORY
(FACTUAL EVIDENCE AND OPINIONS OF CRITICS)

1. *Origin*

a. *Factual Evidence*
The origin of the picture is not known; the first reference to it occurs in 1866; see E. 2, *Subsequent History*.

b. *Opinions concerning Attribution and Date*
Published by *Conway* ([3] 163-164) as Anonymous with various influences; he considered it as the creation of a "syndicate" rather than of an artist. *Winkler* ([6] 371) and *Friedländer* ([9] 105 ff., 137, pl. XLVII-IL; [17] 17 ff. [40] 59 ff., 77, pl. 52-53) ascribed the central panel to the painter called by him the Master of the Legend of S. Catherine and tentatively identified with Pieter van der Weyden (*Friedländer* [9] 108; [40] 60; *Winkler* [20] 468). Both authors gave the *Repose on the Flight to Egypt* to the Magdalen Master (*Friedländer* [9] 106, note ★, 138; [17] 17 f.; [40] 59, note 7, 77; *Winkler* [6] 371; [20] 468; [27] 211), whom *Friedländer* in his vol. VIII (1930, p. 147) suggested is Pieter van Coninxloo.
In 1935 ([17] 17-18), *Friedländer* accepted the opinion of *Hulin de Loo*, published by *Jeanne Tombu* ([12] 262, 281), that the *Marriage at Cana* is by the same hand as the *Flight to Egypt;* in 1926 ([9] 106) *Friedländer* had attributed this to the Master of the Portraits of Princes (whom he later doubtfully amalgamated with the Magdalen Master (*Die Altniederländische Malerei*, Vol. XIV, Leyden, 1937, p. 150). *Winkler* ([27] 211) gave the *Marriage at Cana* to the Magdalen Master. *Reynaud* and *Foucart* ([42] 69) ascribe both faces of this wing to the Magdalen Master.
The right wing obverse and reverse were given to the Master of the Embroidered Foliage by *Friedländer* ([17] 18). For a suggested identification of this master with Monogrammist ADR, see *E. Larsen, The Monogrammist ADR alias the Master with the Embroidered Foliage*, in *Oud-Holland* (Amsterdam), Vol. LXXXVI, 1961, p. 201-2. In *Corpus Pologne* (*Białostocki* [36] 12-13, No. 113), the *Martyrdom of SS. Crispin and Crispinian* (Warsaw) is attributed to the same hand on account of the similarity of the distant rocks and trees (between the tree and the tower on the l.) and the rock and trees in the background of the Melbourne *Raising of Lazarus;* further comparisons are made between the treatment of the nude in both panels, and the facial types. As indicated under D. 1, above, certain plants in *Corpus Pologne* 113 are nearly identical with some in the *S. Peter* here. *Reynaud* and *Foucart* ([42] 68-69) point to a close relationship between S. Peter and the figure of this saint in the *Job altarpiece* (Cologne, Wallraf-Richartz-Museum) on the panel attributed to the Master of S. Barbara; the authors suggest that the Barbara Master when young participated with the Catherine Master in the *Job altarpiece*, later in the *Melbourne retable* and finally carried out alone the retable of the *Martyrdom of SS. Crispin and Crispinian*.
The prominent position of Adolph of Cleves in the *Marriage at Cana* led *Friedländer* to suggest him as the donor who commissioned the picture ([9] 106 note ★★; [17] 18; [40] 59, note 8). This was accepted by subsequent authors except *Bauch* ([33]) and *Vogler* ([14]; see below). *Friedländer* dated the triptych in the first half of the last decade of the 15th century; the *Marriage at Cana*, he thought, must have been commissioned before 1492 (since Adolph

of Cleves died in 1492) and finished before 1496 (since Philip the Fair, who married in 1496, here appears without a wife; *Friedländer* [9] 106-107; [17] 18; [40] 59). *Tombu* ([12] 262) gave the date as ca. 1490; *Glück* ([19] 46) as 'last decade, 15th century'; *Winkler* in 1950 ([27] 211) as ca. 1490 and in 1959 ([31] 185) as 'shortly before 1495'; *Hoff* ([32] 53; [38] 53) as 'commissioned in or before 1492'; *Reynaud* and *Foucart* ([42] 68) as painted about 1495. A different dating was suggested by the following: *Bauch* ([33] 106-7, note 19) suggested that the central panel is a copy of a Dutch painting of about 1460 made in the early 16th century. *Vogler* ([14] 65, 87, note 137) dated the triptych ca. 1510. See also G. *Authors' Comments.*

2. *Subsequent History*

a. *Records concerning Ownership*

1866   In the collection of F. J. Gsell, Vienna, by 1866; recorded by *Waagen* ([1] 316) as "Schule der van Eyck, Altar mit Flügeln. Mitte die Speisung der 5 000 Mann (minder fein)" and description of the other subjects; *Waagen* had not seen the picture himself but reports on information received from *Alfred Woltmann*. *Waagen*'s entry was brought to our attention by Mr. *Lorne Campbell*.

1872   F. J. Gsell Sale, Vienna (Georg Plach), 14.3.1872 (lot 215 as Memlinc); according to *Frimmel* ([2] 95) bought by Sedelmeyer. We are indebted to Dr. *G. Poch-Kalous* for this information.

1922   Sold by Lady Leyland in London through W. H. Romaine Walker, architect, to Mr. Frank Rinder who acquired it under the terms of the Felton Bequest for the National Gallery of Victoria, Melbourne ([4] 83).

1969   Exhibited at Bruges, *Primitifs Flamands Anonymes*, 1969 ([41] No. 45).

b. *Records of Condition and Treatment*

1922   Re-framed by Mr. Draper, National Gallery, London (*Hoff* [32] 50).

1957   'Antiqued' varnish of central panel and obverse of wings removed; and re-varnished by Mr. Harley Griffiths, conservator, National Gallery of Victoria (*Hoff* [32] 60).

F. COMPARATIVE MATERIAL

Central panel
The numbers refer to those on Plate II.

(1) Cf. Mary Magdalene in the *Descent from the Cross*, School of Rogier van der Weyden, Royal Picture Gallery, Mauritshuis, The Hague, No. 264; repr. *M. J. Friedländer, Early Netherlandish Painting*, II, 1967, pl. 68. The connection first mentioned by *de Ricci* ([3] 166).

(7) Cf. drawing claimed to be of Michelle of France, d. 1422, first wife of Philip the Good, in the *Mémoriaux* of Antoine de Succa, I, fol. 11; repr. pl. XLVI. *Devigne* ([11] 343-347) raises doubts about the identity, referring to *A. L. Millin, Antiquités Nationales ou recueil de monumens*, Vol. V, Paris, an VII (1796), fig. numbered 12 on No. LIV (Collégiale Saint-Pierre à Lille), pl. 6, p. 61, where a similar figure (on the tomb of Louis of Male) is called Agnes, Duchess of Bourbon, d. 1476, daughter of John, Duke of Burgundy, 1371-1419, and to another drawing of this figure by *Succa* in a different part of the *Mémoriaux* (fol. 80), Succa calling this figure Isabella of Penthièvre, which *Devigne* thinks right. No identification of this figure by later writers is available.

(10) Cf. portrait on panel now reasonably claimed to be Isabella of Portugal (1397-1471), by Rogier van der Weyden, Estate of the late Mrs. John D. Rockefeller Jr., New York; repr. *E. Panofsky, Early Netherlandish Painting. Its Origins and Character*, Cambridge, Mass., 1953, II, fig. 363. First claimed by *de Ricci* ([3] 166); see also *Belard da Fonseca* ([29] 127-128, figs. 49-50).

(12) Cf. *Portrait drawing of John IV, Duke of Brabant* (1403-1427), Museum Boymans-van Beuningen, Rotterdam; name inscribed; repr. *Panofsky, op. cit.*, II, fig. 380; see his vol. I (p. 291 and note 4). First connected with this figure by *P. Wescher*, 1938 (*Beiträge zu einigen Werken des Kupferstichkabinetts*, in *Berliner Museen*, Berlin, LIX, p. 52-53). Cf. also drawings in the *Mémoriaux* of Antoine de Succa (fol. 11 and 78 v°; pl. XLVI).

(13) Cf. *Portrait drawing of Philip of Brabant* (1405-1430), formerly Mannheimer Coll., Amsterdam, now destroyed; repr. *Panofsky, op. cit.*, fig. 382. Name inscribed. Cf. two drawings in the *Mémoriaux* of Antoine de Succa (fol. 11 and 78 v°; pl. XLVI).

As for the two dogs, cf. *terrier* in the *Legend of S. Catherine* (*Friedländer* [40] pl. 50);

cf. *greyhound* in the l. wing of the *Last Supper* at Bruges (Seminary), attributed to the Catherine Master (*Friedländer* [40] pl. 51).

Left wing, obverse, Marriage at Cana
The numbers refer to those on Plate XII.

(1) Cf. portrait panel of *Philip the Good* (1396-1467), Stedelijk Museum voor Schone Kunsten, Bruges, after a lost original by Rogier van der Weyden (repr. *A. Janssens de Bisthoven*, 1957, *Corpus* No. 13, 110-113, with a list of other versions; cf. also *Friedländer, op. cit.*, II, 1967, No. 125, pl. 127). The connection first mentioned by *de Ricci* ([3] 165).

(2) No prototype known. From the position of this figure to the spectator's left of what is presumably Charles the Bold, she may be one of his wives, and her features bear an approximate resemblance to those in the portrait of Margaret of York (1446-1503) in the Louvre (repr. *Adhémar* [34] *Corpus* No. 79; see also *Michel* [22] 82). *Onghena* ([30] 111) hesitated between Isabella of Bourbon and Margaret of York; *de Ricci* ([3] 165) identified her as Margaret of York with not entirely convincing reference to the drawing in the *Recueil d'Arras* (leaf 64, repr. *de Ricci* [3] pl. II, J.).

(3) From the position among the male figures, following Philip the Good and preceding Maximilian (apparently) and Philip the Fair, this figure would appear to be Charles the Bold, Duke of Burgundy (1433-1477). No prototype is known. Though the face is rounder, the features somewhat resemble those of the portrait usually accepted as by Rogier van der Weyden, Berlin No. 545 (repr. *Friedländer, op. cit.*, II, 1967, No. 42, pl. 65). The rich brocade coat, the chain suggestive of the order of the Golden Fleece, the ermine cap favour this identification. The closest portrait of him is perhaps the one that was in a window (now destroyed) of Notre-Dame, Bruges, repr. pl. XLVII a, from *J. F. Gailliard, Inscriptions funéraires et monumentales de la Flandre Occidentale*, I, Part II, Bruges, 1866, pl. III.

(4) From her position to the r. of Archduke Maximilian (apparently) this would seem to be Mary of Burgundy (1457-1482). No prototype has been found, but there are similarities in the following portraits : similarly cast down eyes occur in a Ms. in the Vienna National Library, Codex 1857, fol. 14 v°, reasonably claimed to be a portrait of Mary of Burgundy (*Pächt* [23] 48-49). The head and position of hand in a stained glass panel, from the Chapel of the Holy Blood, Bruges, at the Victoria and Albert Museum, are comparable (see pl. XLVII b and *B. Rackham, The Stained Glass from the Chapel of the Holy Blood at Bruges, Actes du XIIe Congrès International*

d'Histoire de l'Art, Brussels, 20-29 Sept. 1930, II, 424 ff., pl. XVIII). *De Ricci* ([3] 165) cited the *Recueil d'Arras* drawing (leaf 66), which is not similar (*de Ricci* [3] pl. II, H.).

(5) No prototype known. The long hair and the long nose are characteristic of Maximilian of Austria (1459-1519), appearing for instance in a stained glass panel at the Victoria and Albert Museum from the series referred to above (No. 4, see pl. XLVII c and *ibid.*). For other portraits of Maximilian see *L. Baldass, Der Künstlerkreis Kaiser Maximilians*, 1923. *De Ricci* cited the profile portrait by Ambrogio de Predis in Vienna ([3] 165).

(6) This figure is closely related to the following portraits of Philip the Fair (1478-1506):
   a) drawing, *Recueil d'Arras* (leaf 67); repr. *de Ricci* ([3] pl. II G) and *Onghena* ([30] pl. XXXIII).
   b) panel, Paris, Musée de la Chasse (formerly collection Mrs. Tudor Wilkinson), ca. 1490; repr. *Friedländer* ([17] No. 31, pl. VIII) and *Onghena* ([30] pl. III).
   c) replica of b), Paris, Comte de Montferrand; *Friedländer* ([17] No. 31 a); repr. *Tombu* ([12] 283, fig. 13); see also *Ganz* ([7] Vol. I, 126-127).

(7) This has a certain resemblance to a portrait, dated 1487, of Engelbert II of Nassau (1451-1504), Amsterdam, Rijksmuseum, No. 1538 W1; repr. *Tombu* ([12] 281-2, note 3, fig. 12); *Catalogue of Paintings, Rijksmuseum*, Amsterdam, 1960 (200 f.), Master of the Portraits of Princes.

(8) Cf. portraits of Adolph of Cleves (1425-1492):
   a) drawing, *Recueil d'Arras* (leaf 86), repr. *Winkler* ([31] 187, fig. 7).
   b) panel, formerly T. Harris and Arcade Galleries, London, repr. *Winkler* ([31] 187, fig. 8).
   c) panel, Berlin Museums, on loan to Altena, Westphalia. From an inscription on the back, *Winkler* remarks that this portrait was painted in 1478 ([31] 188, repr. 187, fig. 5); he wears a dress different from that in the Melbourne picture.
   d) panel, collection Prince de Croy, Rumillies, Catalogue of the *Toison d'Or* Exhibition, Bruges, 1962, No. 29, repr.

The identification in the Melbourne Triptych was first made by *Friedländer* ([9] 106).

Right wing, obverse, Raising of Lazarus
The house in the left middle distance is very similar to one in the *Madonna and Child* now in the Johnson Collection, Philadelphia, assigned to the Master of the Embroidered Foliage (*Białostocki* [36] 12; repr. *Friedländer* [40] No. 85, pl. 80; *Cat. of the John G. Johnson Collection*, Philadelphia, 1941, 31, No. 2518; repr. in the *Book of Illustrations*, 1953, 106).

Left wing, reverse, Repose on the Flight to Egypt
The group of the Madonna and Child is related to a half figure *Madonna and Child* in Leningrad, Hermitage, attributed to the Magdalen Master (*Corpus Leningrad*, 1965, No. 112). Many versions or variants of this picture are known and a list is to be found in the Leningrad *Corpus* (p. 64).

The Child may be compared with the Child in a picture in the Cook Collection sale, Christie's, 25 November 1966, lot 58 repr.

The landscape and S. Joseph with the ass are based on Schongauer's engraving of the *Flight to Egypt, Lehrs* [8] No. 7, as set out under D. 1 above.

Right wing, reverse, S. Peter

Comparison may be made with S. Peter (holding one key) in Rogier van der Weyden's *Madonna and Saints*, Frankfurt, Staedelsches Kunstinstitut (*E. Panofsky, Early Netherlandish Painting, op. cit.*, Vol. II, fig. 332). Some plants recur in the *Martyrdom of SS. Crispin and Crispinian*, at Warsaw (see D. 1, p. 9 and *Białostocki* [36] No. 113, 5, a, u and x). The *Sarothamnus scoparius L.* (*Wimmer*), broom, also recurs in the S. *Barbara*, collection Van Wickevoort Crommelin, The Hague (*Białostocki* [36] 12; repr. *Friedländer* [40] No. 86, pl. 81).

G. AUTHORS' COMMENTS

The attribution of the central panel to the Catherine Master seems satisfactory. The delineation of the features is close to those in the panels of the *Legend of S. Catherine* as analyzed by *Friedländer*, 1926 ([9] 103). As *Friedländer* ([9] 105-6) indicates, both types of dogs seen in the picture here occur in the other panels attributed to this master; it is to be noted further that the motif of steps among the rocks to the right in the picture here is similar to that in the upper right hand side of the picture of the *Catherine Legend* (*Friedländer* [40] pl. 50). The X-radiographs (Pl. XL-XLI) reveal a loose handling of the lead paint comparable to that of two panels of a triptych, the *Virgin and Child with SS. Catherine and Barbara* in the Royal Chapel at Granada (*Granada Corpus*, No. 102, pl. CCII, CCVIII and CCXI). The preliminary drawing appearing in the infra-red photograph of the Melbourne picture (Pl. XXXIV) consists of outlines with numerous corrections, as seen, to a lesser degree, in the picture at Granada (*Granada Corpus*, pl. CCIII).

The Magdalen Master is reasonably suggested for the *Repose on the Flight to Egypt*. The face of the Madonna has features related to those in the panels of the *Legend of S. Mary Magdalene* described by *Tombu* ([12] 260) and *Friedländer* ([17] 16). The X-radiograph of a detail of this panel (Pl. XLIV) is hard to read owing to the interference of the composition on the obverse; the lead paint here consists of patches of white perhaps comparable to the *Annunciation* at Granada (*Granada Corpus*, No. 103, pl. CCXVIII. The attribution of this panel has however been doubted, e.g. by *J. Lavalleye, ibid.* p. 125, E.1.b.). Faint outlines of the preliminary drawing appear in the infra-red photograph (Pl. XXXVIII), similar to those in the *Annunciation* cited and in the *Virgin and Child* in the Hermitage Museum at Leningrad (*Corpus Leningrad*, 1965, No. 112, pl. CXVI). The value of comparisons of X-radiographs and infra-red photographs is limited by the small range available at present. The features, types of halo, treatment of hair and other details of the picture here show close family resemblance to *Corpus* No. 112 in Leningrad (see above).

Less convincing is the attribution of the *Marriage at Cana* to the Magdalen Master. The figures here do not show what are described as characteristics of this master's style except in the heads that are based on portraits themselves ascribed to this painter. The lips are not firmly outlined in a strong red but are pale greyish-red with a pale pink outline. The nostrils are not in all heads set rather high in the face. As indicated above, infra-red photographs of works attributed to this master show slight preliminary drawing consisting of outlines principally; in the picture here the preliminary drawing is vigorous and hatching is used in the figure of the bride (Pl. XXXVI-XXXVII). The X-radiograph (Pl. XLII) seems to indicate that the lead white paint is used in a more linear fashion than in the *Repose on the Flight to Egypt* or in *Granada Corpus* No. 103 (see however comment above); note in particular the fingers which here are indicated by one or two outlines, in the other panels by patches of white. *Friedländer* ([17] 15) and *Winkler* ([27] 211) described the Magdalen Master as a Brussels painter, whose work is closely related to Rogier van der Weyden. The *Marriage at Cana*, however, shows characteristics comparable to the work of Dieric Bouts (*Conway* [3] 164). The youth looking through a hatch, the vista into another room and then into a landscape at the back, the servant standing next to a sideboard, the figures of Christ and the Apostles are reminiscent of similar details in the *Last Supper* at Louvain (*M. J. Friedländer, op. cit.*, Vol. III, Leyden/Brussels, 1968, pl. 27). Such Boutsian features are not characteristic of other paintings attributed to the Magdalen Master; to us the attribution of the *Marriage at Cana* to this master remains doubtful. While the main grouping of works under the name of the Catherine Master or the Magdalen Master appears reasonably coherent, we do not feel the same about the works grouped under the name of the Master of the Portraits of Princes whom *Friedländer* in 1926 ([9] 106) suggested for the *Marriage at Cana*. *Reynaud* and *Foucart* ([42] 69) rightly draw attention to the lack of sensibility in the skin surfaces, to the hard folds, the static attitudes, the embarrassed poses of arms and a certain fixity of glances as uncharacteristic of this Master. *Friedländer* doubtfully amalgamated the Master of the Portraits of Princes with the Master of the Magdalen Legend in 1937 (*M. J. Friedländer, op. cit.*, Vol. XIV, Leyden, 1937, p. 150).

The Master of the Embroidered Foliage was reasonably connected with *S. Peter*, r. wing reverse, by *Friedländer* ([17] 18). From photographs it would appear that the treatment of the foliage and plants may be similar here to that in the *Madonna and Child* in the Johnson Collection, Philadelphia (repr. *Friedländer* [40] pl. 80). For the figure of S. Peter and particularly the head no adequately comparable material seems to exist in the work of the Master of the Embroidered Foliage. We agree however with *Reynaud* and *Foucart* ([42] 68) that the square head and the fragile hands bear resemblance to the hands and head in the *Job altarpiece* by the Barbara Master (Cologne, Wallraf-Richartz-Museum; *Friedländer* [40] pl. 64). The infra-red photographs reveal only light outlines and faint shading (Pl. XXXIX).

The attribution (by *Friedländer* [17] 18) of the *Raising of Lazarus* to the same Master of the Embroidered Foliage may have been based in the main on the close correspondence of the castle with one seen in the *Madonna and Child* in the Johnson Collection referred to above. The figures and the landscape, in general, are however too different for a satisfactory comparison to be made. No infra-red or X-ray photographs of other paintings given to this master are known to the authors. The X-radiographs do not reveal any marked difference between the handling of the obverse (Pl. XLIII) and reverse (Pl. XLV) of this panel. The infra-red photograph (Pl. XXXV) of the hands of Lazarus and the bystander differs however markedly from the infra-red photograph of S. Peter's hand (Pl. XXXIX), the parallel shading here occasionally turning into a net of cross hatchings, for instance on the l. hand of Lazarus; lines run around the fingers of the same hand, a feature apparently unusual in 15th century preliminary drawing. The dense parallel shading on the garment contrasts tellingly with the faint outlining of folds on the figure of S. Peter. It seems unlikely that *S. Peter* and the *Raising of Lazarus* are by the same hand.

It is a fact that several highly placed persons, all connected more or less closely with the House of Burgundy, are shown taking part in the scenes in the central panel of this triptych and (even more markedly) in the wing illustrating the *Marriage at Cana*. *Friedländer* has supposed that one of these, Adolph of Cleves, who has the role of the governor of the feast in the *Marriage at Cana*, was the donor of the triptych. To deal first with the first point, there is nothing very unusual in such an inclusion of portraits. Roughly contemporary with the triptych, there are two groups of the *Adoration of the Kings*, assigned to the Master of Frankfurt (*M. J. Friedländer, Early Netherlandish Painting*, VII. *Quentin Massys*, Leyden/Brussels, 1971, Nos. 123, 124, 125; *Art Quarterly*, 1945, Vol. VIII, p. 200, figs. 3, 5a, 5b); some of the examples give recognizable features for one or more of the Kings, in particular the features of the Emperor Frederick III (d. 1493) based on a design popular at the time (for details about this see *A. Scharf's* commentary in the *Catalogue of Pictures and Drawings from the Collection of Sir Thomas Merton, F.R.S.*, London, 1950, No. XXVII; also *H. Dornik-Eger, Friedrich III in Bildnissen und Darstellungen seiner Zeit*, in *Alte und Moderne Kunst* (Vienna), No. 86, May-June 1966, p. 2 ff.). It has been claimed that a similar idea was followed already by Rogier van der Weyden, in whose *Columba altarpiece* at Munich one of the Magi has been thought to have the features of Charles the Bold (*E. Panofsky, Early Netherlandish Painting, op. cit.*, 1953, Vol. I, p. 286). The idea was also followed in the XVth century in Italy, witness Botticelli's *Adoration of the Kings* in the Uffizi, reasonably believed to be the one from Santa Maria Novella in which *Vasari* recorded several portraits of the Medici family, accepted in part by modern writers as correct for the Uffizi picture (*R. Salvini, All the Paintings by Botticelli*, Part I, London, 1965, p. 23, 48 ff., pl. 52). In order to remain fairly close to the Melbourne triptych, examples of portraits of rulers or near-rulers have been cited; others of less highly placed persons could be added.

It is true that we have not found any works, comparable in this respect to the Melbourne triptych, showing the scenes of the *Multiplication* or the *Marriage at Cana*. If no such precisely comparable works exist, we should not feel disturbed, the subject of the *Adoration of the Kings* being in our view near enough.

It seems, on the other hand, very difficult to accept the second point, that one of the portrait figures, Adolph of Cleves, is the donor of the triptych; the evidence that such a thing could happen is indeed by no means so clear as one would wish.

We feel inclined first to comment that Adolph of Cleves in the triptych would be strangely shown if a donor. He turns his back on much of the scene, which includes Christ. Donors in Netherlandish pictures are normally shown reverently kneeling; and this statement, we think, applies to a considerable extent in cases where the figures are merely believed to be donors. Even if they are not kneeling, contemporaries appearing in scenes and believed to have been associated in some way with the commissioning of the pictures seem normally to be shown behaving with propriety; witness Dieric Bouts' *Last Supper* at Louvain where the servants, some of whom are thought to bear the features of the masters of the guild which commissioned the pictures, are humbly arrayed in the background (*J. G. van Gelder*, in *Oud Holland* (Amsterdam), Vol. LXVI, 1951, p. 51-2). A second point is that Adolph of Cleves, unlike the other portraits in the triptych accepted by us, takes an individually named role in the action. We do not think that this must exclude the claim that Adolph was the donor, but would feel more at ease if some historical fact connecting this man and the governor of the feast at the *Marriage at Cana* came to our knowledge.

Another point is that one of the figures in the triptych borrowed from elsewhere is that of the Magdalen from the *Deposition* at The Hague ascribed to Rogier. If (as we incline to think) this figure was merely borrowed as a convenience for the painter, we wonder if the same does not apply to Adolph. This comment applies also in the same degree to the use of Schongauer's engraving in the *Repose*.

A further point concerns the Golden Fleece, which Adolph of Cleves received in 1456. Several of the guests in the *Marriage at Cana*, with the features of Burgundian princes, wear ornaments adapted from the collar of the Golden Fleece, and the fact of these adaptations seems to us evidence against any close connection between the princes and the making of the triptych. The figure with the features of Adolph wears nothing even suggestive of the collar, and we doubt, if he was the donor, whether this even more extreme impropriety could have been committed. Members of the Order were enjoined to wear the collar on every occasion, and it is hard to believe that they would not be shown wearing it in any picture with which they were formally associated. The nearest case we can cite, even remotely suggestive of an exception, is that in a panel portrait of uncertain date, identifiable as *Philip the Fair*, in the Montferrand Collection, where the Golden Fleece has been changed into a pearl, in unknown circumstances (*Tombu* [12] 283, fig. 13; see F. *Comparative Material*, p. 19, 6 c).

Although for these reasons the case for considering Adolph of Cleves the donor is in our view poor, we have not neglected to enquire if other pictures that include the features of contemporaries can be thought analogous to the *Melbourne triptych* with Adolph so considered. The following cases seem to us worth noting in this connection.

First of all, the two groups of the *Adoration of the Kings*, associated with the Master of Frankfurt and referred to previously. It seems most unlikely that all or many of these rather numerous pictures were commissioned by Frederick III. Should one suppose then, that only the first examples of the designs were so commissioned? Then one is admitting that the others, portraits or no, are in some way or other independent. Further, the portrait of Frederick seems to be borrowed from another source and not made for these designs by the Master of Frankfurt (see A. *Scharf* and H. *Dornik-Eger*, as above). Also, one of the compositions of the *Adoration* is itself borrowed from Hugo van der Goes' *Monforte altarpiece*. We do not wish to labour the argument that these pictures offer little or no support for the claim for Adolph in the *Melbourne triptych*.

As for Rogier's *Columba altarpiece*, Charles the Bold was not the donor; it may have been commissioned by Goddert von der Wasservass (M. J. *Friedländer, Early Netherlandish Painting*, II. *Rogier van der Weyden and the Master of Flémalle*, Leyden/Brussels, 1967, p. 69-70, No. 49). Similarly for Botticelli's *Adoration of the Kings;* the donor, it seems, was Giovanni Lami, not any of the Medici. Attempts to find Lami's portrait in the picture have led to figures not well comparable with the prominently participating Adolph of Cleves in the Melbourne picture. Possibly nearer, though still in various ways far, is the Geertgen tot Sint Jans *Story of the Remains of S. John the Baptist*, where founders of the Order of S. John, believed to be portraits of the monks who commissioned the picture, participate in the action of the story, but do not occupy a foreground position like Adolph of Cleves.

A rather more closely comparable case for what has been claimed for Adolph here is a picture of the *Holy Kinship* by Bernard Strigel in Vienna (*Onghena* [30] 131 ff., No. 41, fig. XVI). This picture is claimed to have been painted in 1515 as a straight portrait group of the family of Maximilian. Cuspinian, having acquired it in 1520, had his own family portraits done as a companion piece and holy kinship names added to the heads on both panels (G. *Otto, Bernard Strigel*, Munich/Berlin, 1964, frontispiece, and pl. 97, 144). The rest and main parts of the *Holy Kinship* were painted (without portraits) on the back of the Family of Maximilian, the other panel having inscriptions on the back. Cuspinian, it appears, had no difficulty envisaging New Testament figures with the faces of princely sitters, with the commissioning of the picture involved.

We further particularly mention the Cranach, also of the *Holy Kinship*, dated 1509, at Frankfurt on the Main; it is claimed that this was commissioned by Frederick the Wise of Saxony (Cranach's patron) and Frederick's brother John, and that on the wings Alphaeus is shown with Frederick's features, Zebedee with John's. See M. J. *Friedländer* and J. *Rosenberg, Die Gemälde von Lucas Cranach*, Berlin, 1932, p. 31-2, Nos. 18, 20 (cf. p. 30-1, No. 15). If we had come across any cases more effective than these for supporting the claim of Adolph here as donor, we would have cited them; for us the claim is far from proved, and we must leave the matter so.

Since the members of the House of Burgundy whose portraits are included in the triptych, are, we think, not connected with its commission, we think the dates of the death of Adolph of Cleves (1492) and the marriage of Philip the Fair (1496) of little or no significance for the dating of the picture. As has been stated, the earliest triptychs known to us that can be compared for representing miracles are dated 1461, 1475-1500 and 1499; others must be dated after 1500. The shaped top of our altarpiece is not known to us to occur before 1496 and is much more usual after 1500. *Bauch* assumed that the central panel was a 16th century copy of a Dutch original of about 1460; but we do not see that the central panel differs stylistically very greatly from the rest of the triptych, as it should if the rest is not copied from a similar original. *Friedländer* ([9] 106) suggested that the central panel originally stood alone and that a patron, having acquired it, ordered the wings to be added. Such a development would not be unique and has in fact been claimed for several pictures. For us, a date fairly soon after 1500 is the most probable date; the shape by itself might well suggest 1525; but although old fashioned painting continued to flourish, the style would be noticeably antiquated at so late a date.

The time of origin of the triptych appears not to be clarified by the dates attributed to the painters to whom the various parts are ascribed. *Friedländer* assigned the work of the Catherine Master to between 1470-1500 ([9] 102 f.); he tentatively identified him with Pieter van der Weyden (1437?-1514). *Van Schoute* maintains that the Catherine Master's work has not been sufficiently studied to allow dating within his œuvre (R. *Van Schoute, La Chapelle Royale de Grenade (Les Primitifs flamands, I. Corpus de la peinture des anciens Pays-Bas méridionaux au quinzième siècle*, 6), Brussels, 1963, p. 118).

The pictures more or less certainly assigned to the Master of the Magdalen Legend provide some definite dates. *Friedländer's* earliest date is 1483, the latest 1527 ([17] 15 ff.); he tentatively identified him with Pieter van Coninxloo, who is documented between 1479 and 1513 (*Die Altniederländische Malerei*, VIII. *Jan Gossaert, Bernard van Orley*, Berlin, 1930, p. 146 f.).

The Master of the Embroidered Foliage was assumed by *Friedländer* to have been active before 1500 ([9] 118). Though among the artists concerned only the Magdalen Master is certainly assumed to have worked after 1500, the dates of the Catherine Master and the Master of the Embroidered Foliage are not sufficiently precise to preclude the triptych from having been made soon after 1500.

One may consider whether the date of the triptych can be defined from the costume of the persons shown in it; this question is complicated by the fact that various figures are derived from other works, and some further figures may be similarly derived, although we have not been able to indicate prototypes. Yet it seems correct to say that a date much after 1500 would be in disaccord with the costumes shown.

The presence of historical portraits in the triptych suggests that the painters responsible for them had access to prototypes. Two of the prototypes (Nos. 12 and 13 in the central panel) have been shown above to be connected with statues of ancestors of the House of Burgundy executed as 'plorants' for the Burgundian tombs, claimed by *Panofsky* for Rogier van der Weyden and his workshop (*op. cit.*, p. 291, note 4). *Panofsky* assumes that "in connection with the Burgundian tombs, then, Rogier's workshop must have been commissioned with fairly numerous paintings portraying all the members of the family who were to figure as 'plorants,' paintings of course, the great majority of which had to be copied from originals thirty or forty years old". It seems likely that the painters of the *Multiplication of the Loaves and Fishes* and the *Marriage at Cana* were members of the Rogier workshop or rather of some continuation of this workshop in Brussels.

H. BIBLIOGRAPHY

1866 [1]: G. F. WAAGEN, *Die Vornehmsten Kunstdenkmäler in Wien*, Vienna, 1866.

1914 [2]: THEODOR VON FRIMMEL, *Lexikon der Wiener Gemäldesammlungen, G-L*, Munich, 1914.

1922 [3]: MARTIN CONWAY and SEYMOUR DE RICCI, *A Flemish Triptych for Melbourne*, in *The Burlington Magazine* (London), Vol. XL, 1922, 163-171.

1923 [4]: CHARLES BAGE, *Historical Record of the Felton Bequests from their inception to 31st December 1922*, Melbourne, 1923.

1923 [5]: X., *Illustrated Catalogue of the National Gallery*, Melbourne, 1923.

1924 [6]: FRIEDRICH WINKLER, *Die Altniederländische Malerei. Die Malerei in Belgien und Holland von 1400-1600*, Berlin, 1924.

1925 [7]: P. GANZ, *L'Œuvre d'un amateur d'art. La collection de Monsieur F. Engel-Gros*, 2 vol., Geneva/Paris, (1925).

1925 [8]: MAX LEHRS, *Geschichte und kritischer Katalog der deutschen, niederländischen und französischen Kupferstichs im XV. Jahrhundert. Vierter Abschnitt. Martin Schongauer und seine Schule*, Vienna, 1925.

1926 [9]: MAX J. FRIEDLÄNDER, *Die Altniederländische Malerei, IV. Hugo van der Goes*, Berlin, 1926.

1927 [10]: MARTIN CONWAY, *The Literature of Art. Dr. Friedländer on Van der Goes* [...], in *The Burlington Magazine* (London), Vol. L, 1927, 220-221.

1927 [11]: MARGUERITE DEVIGNE, *Une Collection d'œuvres d'art à Tournai au commencement du XVIIe siècle*, in *Fédération archéologique et historique de Belgique. Annales du XXIVe Congrès* (Tournai 1921), Tournai, 1927, 341-363.

1929 [12]: JEANNE TOMBU, *Le Maître de la Légende de Marie-Madeleine*, in *Gazette des Beaux-Arts* (Paris), 6th ser., Vol. II, 1929, 258-291.

1929 [13]: FIERENS-GEVAERT and PAUL FIERENS, *Histoire de la peinture flamande des origines à la fin du XVe siècle, III. La Maturité de l'art flamand*, Paris/Brussels, 1929.

1930 [14]: KARL VOGLER, *Die Ikonographie der "Flucht nach Aegypten,"* Inauguraldissertation, Heidelberg, 1930.

1932 [15]: E. LA TOUCHE ARMSTRONG and R. D. BOYS, *The Book of the Public Library, Museums and National Gallery of Victoria, 1906-1931*, Melbourne, 1932.

1933 [16]: K. SMITS, *De Iconografie van de Nederlandsche Primitieven*, Amsterdam/Brussels/Antwerp/Louvain, 1933.

1935 [17]: MAX J. FRIEDLÄNDER, *Die Altniederländische Malerei, XII. Pieter Coeck. Jan van Scorel*, Leyden, 1935.

1941 [18]: PAUL WESCHER, *Das höfische Bildnis von Philipp dem Guten bis zu Karl V*, in *Pantheon* (Munich), Vol. XXVIII, 1941, 195-202, 272-277.

1942 [19]: GUSTAV GLÜCK, *The Feeding of the Five thousand in the Painting of the Netherlands*, in *The Art Quarterly* (Detroit), Vol. V, 1942, 45-57.

1942 [20]: FRIEDRICH WINKLER, *Weyden, Peter (Pieret) van der*, in *Allgemeines Lexikon der bildenden Künstler von der Antike bis zur Gegenwart* (begründet von ULRICH THIEME und FELIX BECKER), Leipzig, XXXV, 1942, 468.

1943 [21]: X., *Catalogue of the National Gallery of Victoria*, Melbourne, 1943.

1944 [22]: EDOUARD MICHEL, *L'Ecole flamande du XVe siècle au Musée du Louvre*, Brussels, 1944.

1948 [23]: OTTO PÄCHT, *The Master of Mary of Burgundy*, London, (1948).

1948 [24]: X., *Catalogue of the National Gallery of Victoria*, Melbourne, 1948.

1949 [25]: MAX J. FRIEDLÄNDER, *Der Meister der Katharinen-Legende und Rogier van der Weyden*, in *Oud-Holland* (Amsterdam), Vol. LXIV, 1949, 156-161.

1950 [26]: P. Bautier, R. Cazier, R. L. Delevoy, Ch. De Mayer, P. Fierens and E. Greindl, *Dictionnaire des Peintres*, Brussels, [1950].

1950 [27]: Friedrich Winkler, *Meister der Magdalenen-Legende*, in *Allgemeines Lexikon der bildenden Künstler von der Antike bis zur Gegenwart* (begründet von Ulrich Thieme und Felix Becker), Leipzig, XXXVII, 1950, 211.

1950 [28]: X., *Meister der Fürstenbildnisse*, in *Allgemeines Lexikon der bildenden Künstler von der Antike bis zur Gegenwart* (begründet von Ulrich Thieme und Felix Becker), Leipzig, XXXVII, 1950, 109.

1957 [29]: António Belard da Fonseca, *O Misterio dos Painéis*, Lisbon, 1957.

1959 [30]: M. J. Onghena, *De Iconografie van Philips de Schone* (*Académie royale de Belgique. Classe des Beaux-Arts. Mémoires. Collection in-8°.* Tome X), Brussels, 1959.

1959 [31]: Friedrich Winkler, *Zur Kenntnis und Würdigung des Jan Mostaert*, in *Zeitschrift für Kunstwissenschaft* (Berlin), Vol. XIII, 1959, 177-214.

1961 [32]: Ursula Hoff, *Catalogue of European Paintings before Eighteen Hundred. National Gallery of Victoria*, Melbourne, 1961.

1961-2 [33]: Kurt Bauch, *Bildnisse des Jan van Eyck*, in *Sitzungsbericht der Heidelberger Akademie der Wissenschaften. Jahresheft 1961/62* (Heidelberg), 1963, 96-142.

1962 [34]: Hélène Adhémar, *Le Musée national du Louvre. Paris* (*Les Primitifs flamands*, I. *Corpus de la peinture des anciens Pays-Bas méridionaux au quinzième siècle*, 5), I, Brussels, 1962.

1965 [35]: Hans Aurenhammer, *Brotvermehrung*, in *Lexikon der Christlichen Ikonographie*, Part 5, Vienna, 1965, 409-419.

1966 [36]: Jan Białostocki, *Les Musées de Pologne (Gdańsk, Kraków, Warszawa)* (*Les Primitifs flamands*, I. *Corpus de la peinture des anciens Pays-Bas méridionaux au quinzième siècle*, 9), Brussels, 1966.

1966 [37]: Gertrud Schiller, *Ikonographie der christlichen Kunst*, Vol. I. *Inkarnation, Kindheit, Taufe, Versuchung, Verklärung, Wirken und Wunder Christi*, Gütersloh, 1966.

1967 [38]: Ursula Hoff, *Catalogue of European Paintings before Eighteen Hundred. National Gallery of Victoria*, 2nd, enlarged ed., Melbourne, 1967.

1968 [39]: U. Nilgen, *Brotvermehrung*, in *Lexikon der christlichen Ikonographie* (herausgegeben von Engelbert Kirschbaum), I, Rome/Freiburg/Basel/Vienna, 1968, 326-330.

1969 [40]: Max J. Friedländer, *Early Netherlandish Painting*, IV. *Hugo van der Goes*, Leyden/Brussels, 1969.

1969 [41]: *Primitifs flamands anonymes [...]. Exposition organisée par la Ville de Bruges au Groeningemuseum. 14 juin-21 septembre 1969*, Bruges, 1969.

1970 [42]: Nicole Reynaud and Jacques Foucart, *Expositions. Primitifs flamands anonymes*, in *Revue de l'Art* (Paris), No. 8, 1970, 66-72.

J. LIST OF PLATES

No. 131: ANONYMOUS (13)

I.	The Triptych with the Miracles of Christ Central panel, *The Multiplication of the Loaves and Fishes*	N. G. 10 025 E 1965
II.	The figures and plants mentioned in the text	R. Versteegen, Brussels
III.	The whole	N.G. 10 026 E 1965

IV.	The lower left corner	N.G.	10 043 E	1965
V.	The lower right corner	N.G.	10 045 E	1965
VI.	The group of Christ and the Apostles in the middle distance on the right	N.G.	10 046 E	1965
VII.	The multitude in the middle distance on the left and the miracles in the background	N.G.	10 044 E	1965
VIII.	God the Father with Angels (1:1)	N.G.	10 050 E	1965
IX.	Six persons sitting on the right (1:1)	N.G.	10 049 E	1965
X.	Busts of Jacoba of Bavaria (?) and John IV, Duke of Brabant (M 2×)	N.G.	10 047 E	1965
XI.	Busts of Philip of Saint Pol, Duke of Brabant and of a woman (M 2×)	N.G.	10 048 E	1965

Left wing, obverse, *The Marriage at Cana*

XII.	a) The whole	N.G.	10 077 E	1965
	b) The figures identified in the text	R. Versteegen, Brussels		
XIII.	The upper half	N.G.	10 032 E	1965
XIV.	The lower half	N.G.	10 033 E	1965
XV.	Detail showing Philip the Fair and the table (1:1)	N.G.	10 030 E	1965
XVI.	The three wives of Philip the Good (1:1 approx.)	N.G.	10 034 E	1965
XVII.	Engelbert II of Nassau (?) and Adolph of Cleves (1:1)	N.G.	10 031 E	1965
XVIII.	Philip the Good, Charles the Bold and Margaret of York (?) (1:1)	N.G.	10 035 E	1965
XIX.	Detail of architecture showing two niches with the serpent and Adam and Eve after the Fall	N.G.	10 036 E	1965

Right wing, obverse, *The Raising of Lazarus*

XX.	a) The whole	N.G.	10 028 E	1965
	b) The figures and plants identified in the text	R. Versteegen, Brussels		
XXI.	The lower half	N.G.	10 054 E	1965
XXII.	Busts of Christ, a woman and some disciples	N.G.	10 053 E	1965
XXIII.	The house and the landscape in the background	N.G.	10 055 E	1965

XXIV.	The Reverse of the Triptych	N.G.	10 029 E	1965
		ACL	214 155 B	1965

Left wing, reverse, *The Repose on the Flight to Egypt*

XXV.	The Virgin, Child and landscape	N.G.	10 052 E	1965
XXVI.	The Child	N.G.	10 051 E	1965
XXVII.	Detail of the landscape, infra-red	ACL	L 5 932 E	1965

Right wing, reverse, *S. Peter*

XXVIII.	The upper part with the bust of S. Peter	N.G.	10 042 E	1965
XXIX.	The middle part with the hands of S. Peter	N.G.	10 038 E	1965
XXX.	The plants identified in the lower part	R. Versteegen, Brussels		
XXXI.	The lower part	N.G.	10 039 E	1965

XXXII.	Bust of S. Peter	N.G.	10 041 E	1965
XXXIII.	Detail of the plants	N.G.	10 040 E	1965
XXXIV.	Detail of the central panel, infra-red	ACL	L 5 926 E	1965
XXXV.	Detail of the right wing obverse, infra-red	ACL	L 5 931 E	1965
XXXVI.	Detail of the left wing obverse, infra-red	ACL	L 5 929 E	1965
XXXVII.	Detail of the left wing obverse, infra-red	ACL	L 5 928 E	1965
XXXVIII.	Detail of the left wing reverse, infra-red	ACL	L 5 933 E	1965
XXXIX.	Detail of the right wing reverse, infra-red	ACL	L 5 934 E	1965
XL.	Detail of the central panel, X-radiograph (1:1)	ACL	L 478 C	1965
XLI.	Detail of the central panel, X-radiograph (1:1)	ACL	L 477 C	1965
XLII.	Detail of the left wing obverse, X-radiograph (1:1)	ACL	L 479 C	1965
XLIII.	Detail of the right wing obverse, X-radiograph (1:1)	ACL	L 481 C	1965
XLIV.	Detail of the left wing reverse, X-radiograph (1:1)	ACL	L 480 C	1965
XLV.	Detail of the right wing reverse, X-radiograph (1:1)	ACL	L 482 C	1965

Comparative Material

XLVI.   *Mémoriaux* of Antoine de Succa, Brussels, Bibliothèque Royale Albert Ier,
Ms. II 1862, I, f⁰ 11   Bibliothèque Royale

XLVII.   a) Charles the Bold, stained glass panel (now destroyed) of Notre-Dame,
Bruges (from J. F. GAILLIARD, *Inscriptions funéraires et monumentales de*   ACL 128 551 A 1971
la Flandre occidentale, I, Part II, Bruges, 1866, pl. III)

         b) Mary of Burgundy, stained glass panel from the Chapel of the Holy   Victoria and Albert
Blood, Bruges (London, Victoria and Albert Museum)   Museum

         c) Maximilian of Austria, stained glass panel from the Chapel of the   Victoria and Albert
Holy Blood, Bruges (London, Victoria and Albert Museum)   Museum

XLVIII.   a) The Reverse of the central panel   ACL 214 131 B 1965

132

A. CLASSIFICATION IN THE CORPUS

No. 132: GROUP EYCK (9), *THE MADONNA AND THE CHILD*

B. IDENTIFYING REFERENCES

Follower of van Eyck
The Madonna and the Child
No. 1275/3 in the *Catalogue of European Paintings before Eighteen Hundred, National Gallery of Victoria*, Melbourne, 1967 ([79] 46-49).

C. PHYSICAL CHARACTERISTICS

(By A. Philippot and R. V. Sneyers on the basis of the report "Examen de laboratoire de la Vierge d'Ince Hall" by P. Coremans, A. Philippot and R. V. Sneyers, dated 14th November 1958)

Forme: parfaitement rectangulaire.

Dimensions: 26,4×19,5×0,7 cm.

Couche protectrice: mince couche de vernis à base de résine synthétique.

Couche picturale: dans un état satisfaisant; usure très inégale du bord des craquelures (pl. LI), particulièrement marquée au voisinage du texte de gauche (pl. LX) et sur le plancher à l'avant-plan; retouches anciennes des lacunes bordant les craquelures que certaines retouches bouchent; restaurations le long du bord supérieur, sur le plancher et au bas du bord de droite.

Absence de bords non peints et de barbes, mais présence aux bords supérieur et gauche du tableau d'un sillon net, étroit, parallèle aux bords du tableau et creusant la couche picturale (pl. LIVa) dont la lisière a l'aspect caractéristique d'une entaille faite dans une matière tendre, non friable, comme l'est une peinture relativement fraîche (pl. LIVb). Reprise du dessin interne de l'hélix de l'oreille de la Vierge, retouches au chandelier, surpeints de détails sur le tapis, sur le bahut et ses éléments métalliques, sur la bande brunâtre de fond séparant le bahut du drap de majesté.

Les retouches bouchant localement des lacunes et des craquelures et certaines retouches ou 'touches' de couleur observées sur des plages intactes du tableau, notamment au visage et à la chevelure de la Vierge (pl. LXII), au visage et aux contours ombrés des jambes de l'Enfant, au bahut et au tapis, résistent aux solvants comme les couches picturales originales.

1. *Craquelures*

La maille des craquelures est du type rectangulaire à sens dominant horizontal; cette maille est uniforme sur toute la surface de la peinture; elle ne change ni de dimensions ni de forme suivant les différentes structures et compositions picturales et forme un réseau de mosaïque indépendant de la peinture. Le tracé des craquelures n'est pas net mais "zigzague" en maints endroits; il donne moins l'impression d'une craquelure d'âge que d'une rupture de pâte incomplètement durcie (pl. LIVb). La préparation anormalement épaisse et très fortement chargée de colle serait à l'origine de cette craquelure à maille continue et dont le sens préférentiel est contraire au fil du bois.

En divers endroits, notamment à la tablette brunâtre du bahut, à la base du chandelier et dans le manteau rouge, les craquelures sont bouchées par des agglomérats informes qui offrent la même résistance aux solvants que la peinture originale.

2. *Composition et structure des couches picturales analysées*

Avant la restauration de 1958, la matière picturale originale était isolée des retouches anciennes et du vernis assez épais, jauni et craquelé, par un film de matière transparente que le Scientific Department de la National Gallery de Londres identifia comme une protéine similaire au blanc d'œuf (pl. LXIII). M. A. Philippot, Restaurateur en chef de l'Institut royal du Patrimoine artistique à Bruxelles, enleva ce film par grattage après que les retouches et le vernis dégradé eussent été éliminés par action rapide de solvants auxquels par ailleurs la couche originale résista parfaitement. Une couche transparente de cette nature n'a jamais été identifiée jusqu'à présent sur les tableaux flamands du XVᵉ siècle. M. F. I. G. Rawlins fit remarquer que l'application d'une telle couche sur une couleur à l'huile incomplètement sèche constitue un excellent moyen de production de craquelures artificielles.

Le liant de la peinture originale est généralement huileux; il résiste aux solvants.

Bleu de la robe de la Vierge, en deux couches: une couche à base de lapis-lazuli et d'un peu de blanc de plomb, couverte d'un glacis à base de lapis-lazuli et d'un liant aqueux.

Vert du baldaquin, en trois couches: une couche grisâtre de blanc de plomb et noir animal, couverte d'une première couche verte de malachite, peu de lapis-lazuli et de blanc de plomb et d'une couche verte rendue plus claire par addition de blanc de plomb.

Jaune de la fenêtre, à base d'oxyde double de plomb et d'étain.

Rouge du manteau de la Vierge, en deux couches: l'inférieure à base de vermillon et de garance, la supérieure au glacis de garance.

Rouge des franges du baldaquin, en une couche, tantôt à base de garance, tantôt de vermillon ou de garance et vermillon.

Bruns du fond du tapis et du bahut, en une couche composée d'ocre brune, de noir animal et de blanc de plomb en proportions diverses.

Noir des ombres du manteau de la Vierge, en une couche à base de noir animal appliqué à la détrempe.

Blanc des chairs, en une couche à base de blanc de plomb et d'un peu de vermillon.

Ces compositions et structures ne correspondent pas à ce que l'on observe généralement sur les œuvres du XVᵉ siècle flamand où le *bleu* a couramment pour couche de fond de l'azurite liée à l'huile, le *vert* n'est pas composé de lapis-lazuli mais de malachite recouverte d'un glacis au résinate de cuivre et l'*ombre des rouges* y est obtenue par application d'un épais glacis de garance.

Par contre, le jaune à base d'oxyde de plomb et d'étain est un matériau généralement considéré comme caractéristique des tableaux flamands des XVᵉ et XVIᵉ siècles.

3. *Dessin préparatoire et exécution picturale*

Le dessin de mise en place de la composition apparaît à la manche et à la ceinture de la Vierge, au bord inférieur de la robe visible dans l'ouverture du manteau et en quelques points du contour du manteau (pl. LII). Les nombreux débordements des couches picturales sous-jacentes, notamment le vert du baldaquin que l'on retrouve sous le fond brunâtre, caractérisent une exécution peu précise et font songer à une imitation superficielle.

Plusieurs plis et contours du manteau de la Vierge (pl. LVIII et LIXa) sont exécutés au blanc de plomb couvert d'un léger glacis rouge, alors que la technique usuelle de van Eyck et des maîtres flamands du XVe siècle rend le modelé par superposition de glacis.

Changements de composition: surélévation de la fenêtre (pl. L) et élargissement du bleu de la robe dans l'ouverture du manteau (pl. LII).

Préparation: blanchâtre, à base de craie et de colle animale, formant une couche allant jusqu'à 700 μ d'épaisseur très fortement imprégnée d'huile, en excellent état. L'épaisseur des préparations des maîtres flamands du XVe siècle va de 100 à 400 μ.

Support: un élément vertical de chêne d'Europe centrale, débité plein quartier, d'épaisseur inégale, en excellent état. Le revers taillé à la plane, est teinté d'un lavis gris-noir. Les bords horizontaux sont sciés et les bords verticaux rabotés au ras de la surface peinte; ils ne sont pas patinés. Des languettes de chêne, clouées sur la tranche du panneau, portent les dimensions de l'ensemble à 27,7 × 20,7 cm.

On ne connaît pas de tableau de chevalet flamand du XVe siècle sans bord non peint ni barbe sur le pourtour du panneau.

Marques au revers: sceau de cire rouge apposé à même la teinture noirâtre; le sceau n'a pu être identifié malgré des recherches (pl. LXVIIIb).

Cadre: moderne.

D. DESCRIPTION AND ICONOGRAPHY

1. *Subject*
(see also I, *doc.* 1, *Davies*, p. 46)

The Virgin is clad in a plain mantle and a dress bordered with jewels at the neckline and white fur trimmings at the cuffs and hem of the skirt, held at the waist by a belt studded with gold. Her hair, which falls over her shoulders, is held back by a ribbon decorated with pearls, with a ringlet of pearls at the centre. She sits on a low bench in front of a cloth of honour surmounted by a baldachin in a room dimly lit from the left by a window. A carpet lies in front of the cloth of honour. Turning to the left the Virgin holds with both hands an illuminated manuscript which rests on the lap of the Christ Child seated on her right knee. The Child turns over the pages.

Inside the window opening appear the hinges and part of a shutter opening outward; above some leadlights which reflect their shadows on the reveal. On the sill two oranges. Below a bench which continues to the back wall; on it a glass jar with stopper, half filled with water; in front a half round shadow as if cast by an object outside the picture. Another bench runs along the back wall. On the right a cupboard with keys hanging from the keyhole. On top a brass pricket chandelier with taper and two sconce branches next to a silver or pewter ewer with brass mountings. A brass basin stands on the floor in front of the cabinet.

The Madonna seated close to the ground, in a domestic interior yet under a regal baldachin is a combination of the "Madonna of Humility" and the "Queen of Heaven", cf. *Beenken* ([57] 66-67), *Panofsky* ([61] I, 183); *Meiss* ([73] 278). A comparable combination, quoted by *Panofsky* ([61] I, 61, 183, II, fig. 67), occurs in the *Adoration of the Magi* in the illumination by the Boucicaut Master in the *Très Belles Heures du Maréchal de Boucicaut*, 1400-1410 A.D.

The "Madonna of Humility" in a domestic interior without the cloth of honour appears repeatedly in the work of the Flémalle Master; comparison may be made with the *Madonna at the Fireplace, Corpus Leningrad* [77] 8, No. 108; *Tolnay* ([51] 25), *Baldass* ([60] 51). Ewer, basin, candlestick and glass bottle are interpreted by *Panofsky* as symbols of the purity of the Virgin and the pieces of fruit as signifying the 'gaudia Paradisi' ([61] I, 143, 144). The open book as an accessory of the Child is rare before the 15th century. D. C. *Shorr* (*The Christ Child in Devotional Images in Italy during the XIVth century*, New York, 1954, 189), describes only one type under No. 34, "the Child seated on the Virgin's knee. He directs his head and glance downwards at the book held by the Virgin and points to the words with his right forefinger". In van Eyck's picture here the Child is seated behind the book and grasps a leaf with each hand. Apart from versions quoted under F. directly connected with No. 132, the following may be compared: a Child behind the book occurs in the *Holy Family with SS. Catherine and Barbara* at Naples (Museo Nazionale), thought to be from the school of Konrad Witz (ca. 1410-ca. 1445); see *Burckhardt* ([23] 194), *Phillips* ([29] 104), *Wendland* ([46] 97) and *Schmid* ([58] 152). Repr. in J. Gantner, *Konrad Witz*, 2nd ed., Vienna, 1943, pl. 1-3.

The motif of the Child handling the book appears transformed in the *Durán Madonna* (Madrid, Prado) by Rogier van der Weyden, dated ca. 1437 by *Panofsky* ([61] I, 259, II, fig. 317). A late example of the Child behind the book occurs in three early Madonnas by Quentin Massys (1465/6-1530): 1, 2. *Virgin and Child Enthroned*, Brussels (Musées royaux des Beaux-Arts), M. J. Friedländer, *Early Netherlandish Painting*, VII. *Quentin Massys*, Leyden/Brussels, 1971, Nos. 17, 20, pl. 22, 25; 3. *The Virgin and Child enthroned with four Angels*, London, *National Gallery Acquisitions, 1953-1962*, (London, 1962), 60, No. 6282, repr. Another example is Colyn de Coter, *Madonna*, Chicago (The Art Institute), M. J. Friedländer, *Early Netherlandish Painting*, IV. *Hugo van der Goes*, Leyden/Brussels, 1969, pl. 91.

2. *Colours*

The Virgin is in a blue dress and a red mantle; her hair is light brown. Red and blue stones decorate the neckline. The hair of the Christ Child is fair. The brocade of the cloth of honour and the baldachin are green embossed brocade woven with a gold pattern. The walls of the room are grey, the furniture brown; yellow and muddy red appear in the carpet.

3. *Inscriptions and Heraldry*

Inscribed on the back wall to left of canopy C̄OPLETV̄ ĀNO D MCCCCXXXIIJ° P JOHEM DE EYC BRVGIS (CO[M]PLETV[M] A[N]NO D[OMINI] MCCCCXXXIIJ P[ER] JOH[ANN]EM DE EYC BRVGIS) (Pl. LX) and on right hand side: AΛC IXA XAN (Pl. LXI).

As pointed out in *Davies'* report (section I, *doc.* 1) the following features of the inscription are faulty:

a) The last letter of the second word of the motto should be an *H;*

b) The spelling of the name as *Eyc* is strange;

c) The form $\overline{Ano}$ *D* instead of $\overline{Ano}$ *DNI* or $\overline{ANO}$ *D*[I] is unusual;

d) To begin the word *CŌPLETV* without the usual abbreviation for *con* or *com* (?) seems to be unusual in van Eyck's work.

Held ([64] 217) drew attention to the fact that the date is written in Roman numerals, contrary to Jan's general practice of using Arabic ones, or – exceptionally – a combination of both, but his argument has lost weight since in 1955 the inscription on the frame of the *Virgin* in Dresden was found to have been written in Roman numerals: MºCCCCºXXXVij.

The form of the inscription does not recur quite like this among van Eyck's signatures. Particularly the word *BRVGIS* does not appear in signatures which are held to be authentic. See also E.1.b and G. *Author's Comments*.

On the back of the panel, the arms (Pl. LXVIII b), not yet identified, belonged to an ecclesiastic. The red sealing-wax stamp shows: "Per pale Christ's apparition (?) standing upon a terrace and a fruicted eradicated tree surmonted by a mullet of six points, the base wavy". There is no reason to deny a Sicilian, Italian or Spanish origin of this stamp, as the wavy base is particularly frequent in these regions.

E. ORIGIN AND SUBSEQUENT HISTORY
(FACTUAL EVIDENCE AND OPINIONS OF CRITICS)

1. *Origin*

a. *Factual Evidence*

Nothing is known of the origin of this picture. No contemporary document concerning the origin is known except the inscription, the authenticity of which is questioned, cf. E.2, *Subsequent History*.

b. *Opinions concerning Attribution and Date*

Since the authenticity of the inscription has been questioned more frequently than that of the painting itself, the two are here discussed separately.

The inscription

While many authors have accepted the signature as authentic, doubts were expressed early. In 1892, *Leprieur* ([11] 170) published a criticism in which the inscription was described as unauthentic, possibly copied from the frame, by a copyist who imitated without comprehension. *Leprieur* mentions the bizarre form of some of the letters, their placing into a space too narrow for them, the cutting short of certain words as uncharacteristic for Jan van Eyck. *Tschudi* ([12] 101) commented on the "childish and uncertain nature" of the letters of the inscription. *Bode* ([18] 122) supposed the inscription to be overpainted. *Friedländer* ([17] 475; [24] 574, No. 3; [34] 130) assumed that the inscription was unauthentic and put on the picture at a later date, presumably taken from van Eyck's inscription on the original frame. He abandoned his doubts of the inscription in 1924 ([44] 53-54; [78] 39-40) since the restorer *Zink* ([41] 4) affirmed that it was coeval with the main paint layer. *Panofsky* ([61] 183 note 1) returned to *Friedländer's* earlier argument assuming the inscription to be unauthentic and taken from the original frame. *Held* ([64] 217) questioned the fact that "the date is written in Roman numerals, contrary to Jan's general practice of using Arabic ones or – exceptionally – a combination of both". *Pächt* ([65] 274, note 32) and *Grossmann* ([68] 3-4) took the inscription to be unauthentic. The investigations made at the Institut royal du Patrimoine artistique in 1958 (see section I, p. 45) reaffirmed *Zink*'s observation that the painting and the inscription are of the same date and by the same hand.

Date

Waagen ([3] 249; [4] I, 87), *Crowe* and *Cavalcaselle* ([5] 122) and *Schnaase* and *Eisenmann* ([7] 144) had read the date as 1432; *Tschudi* ([12] 101-102) read 1433; *Weale*, who had quoted 1432 in 1883 ([9] 193), corrected his reading to 1433 in 1906 ([27] 185); the earlier date however continued to be read, as for example by *Held* ([64] 217) and *Grossmann* ([68] 3-4); the latter considered it possible, that the original date read MCCCCXXVIII, misread by the copyist as MCCCCXXXIII.

Fürbringer ([33] 36-39) and *Schmarsow* ([45] 100-103), commenting on the discrepancy between the gothic rhythm of the figure and the cramped interior, assumed the figure to have been begun before 1432 or 1433. *Musper* ([59] 104) referred to the style of the picture as 'retardataire' for 1433. *Pächt* ([65] 274, note 32) and by verbal communication to the author in 1959 and *Grossmann* ([68] 3-4) drew in doubt the accuracy of the reading of the date (see above); *Grossmann* regarded an earlier date as more appropriate to the style of the picture. *Baldass* ([60] 277) and *Panofsky* ([61] I, 183) accepted 1433 as the correct reading.

The painting

While accepting No. 132 as an original by Jan van Eyck, *Tschudi* ([12] 101) was the first to draw attention to a lack of quality in the detail of the painting: "Die Nebendinge sind etwas flüchtig behandelt, das Muster auf dem Teppich hinter der Madonna wirkt unruhig"; he also noted retouching. *Tschudi*'s comments were repeated by *Kaemmerer* ([14] 58-60); *Voll* ([16] 87-89) rejected the painting (without however having first hand knowledge of it) considering it to be a copy from an original by van Eyck. *Friedländer* ([17] 475) accepted the painting as genuine. *Bode* ([18] 122) considered No. 132 though, he thought, badly overpainted, to be the original from which the versions in the Verdura Collection and at Catania were copied (cf. F. *Comparative Material*, 1, 2). *Durand-Gréville* ([21] 34-35) who knew No. 132 from a photograph, believed that it was by Hubert van Eyck, remained unfinished at Hubert's death and was finished by Jan. *Friedländer* ([24] 574) thought that the picture was disfigured by old retouches and opaque varnish, but felt that in some parts the art of van Eyck in drawing and colour was sufficiently in evidence for it to be regarded as an original. Later authors followed *Friedländer*'s assessment. After the acquisition by Melbourne in 1922, writers had no personal knowledge of No. 132 until it was exhibited in the United States between 1939 and 1941. Having examined the original, *Panofsky* ([61] I, 183) regarded the face of the Madonna as partially repainted. *Pächt* ([65] 274, note 32) implied a doubt of the authenticity of the work on account of the transition from the thorax to the knee section in the figure of the Virgin (which does not, so he thought, recur like this in authentic pictures by van Eyck) and on account of the serpentine movement of the main current of the folds and the lack of precision in the sitting posture.

In 1957-8, No. 132 was examined at the Institut royal du Patrimoine artistique in Brussels (Sections C, E.2.b, and I) by Dr. *Paul Coremans* and members of his Institute in collaboration with Mr. *Rawlins* and his staff of the London National Gallery Laboratory as well as Mr. *Martin Davies*. The examiners came to the conclusion that the picture was an old copy after a lost original by Jan van Eyck. A short *résumé* of the findings was published by the author in 1961 ([72] 47-48). Dr. *Panofsky* who kindly agreed to examine the photographs and reports from the Institut royal du Patrimoine artistique at the request of Trustees and Director of the National Gallery of Victoria, agreed with the findings (letter Princeton, 24.II.1959 to *Eric Westbrook*, Director, National Gallery of Victoria). *Meiss* ([73] 310, note 12) had examined the documents from Brussels together with

Dr. *Panofsky;* accepting the conclusions drawn by the Institut, *Meiss* stressed the aesthetic inferiority of No. 132 in comparison to the, similar, *S. Barbara* of 1437 at Antwerp (Kon. Museum voor Schone Kunsten).

2. *Subsequent History*

a. *Records concerning Ownership*

The seal on the back of No. 132 recorded in section C, described in section D.3 and by *Weale* ([9] 193, note 1), has not been identified (Pl. LXVIII b).

For a seventeenth century inscription concerning a pledge, often referred to in connection with No. 132, see F. *Comparative Material,* No. 1.

1803	In 1961 ([72] 49, note 2) I wrote that No. 132 could be identical with a note in an inventory of pictures at Ince Hall of 1803 ([1]), No. CXVI „*THE VIRGIN AND CHILD. The great merit of this picture consists in its being a very ancient painting as appears by the name and date on it. It is much in the style of Albert Duerer and shows the progress of the arts*". *Jacob* ([70] 7, 8) however, states that the comment quoted above refers to a painting by Dirk Bouts, and confirms this in 1967 when a double-sided picture of the *Virgin and Child,* with a *Portrait of a Young Man* (unfinished) on the verso, was shown in the Russel-Cotes exhibition of the Weld-Blundell pictures at Bournemouth No. 82, under the attribution 'Manner of Dieric Bouts', signed and dated 1490; this picture still had the number 116 on the label at the time of exhibition. I am indebted to Mr. *Jacob* and Mr. *Davies* for this information. *Jacob* ([70] 8) suggests that the van Eyck was acquired by Henry Blundell in the last seven years of his life (he died 1810), when he was nearly blind, possibly with the assistance of William Roscoe (1753-1831). *Jacob* quotes an entry in *The Farington Diary* of June 26, 1806 (ed. James Greig, London, 1924, III, 262) stating that Henry Blundell "*granted an annuity of £500 a year to a person aged 52 or 53 for a collection of works of art*". Blundell's collection increased from 197 pictures in 1803 to 314 listed in an inventory taken on Charles Blundell's death in 1841; *Jacob* states that there is no reason to suppose that Charles was responsible for the additions.
1850	The picture was identified as by Jan van Eyck by *Waagen* on his visit to Ince Hall in 1850 ([3] 249) when he saw it hanging in the chaplain's room.
1853	*Waagen* ([3] 249) may well have meant *Förster* ([2] 67) when he referred to a friend having told him that the van Eyck was now hanging in the Drawing Room at Ince Hall.
1863	Seen by *Crowe* and *Cavalcaselle* at Ince Hall ([5] 121-123).
1883	Seen by *Weale* at Ince Hall ([9] 193) and apparently also by *Stevenson* ([8] 440).
1884	Exhibited at the Royal Academy Winter Exhibition, London, in 1884, No. 267.
1892	Exhibited at the Guild Hall, London, 1892, No. 48.
1892	Exhibited at the Burlington Fine Arts Club, London, 1892, No. 14 A.
1906	Exhibited at the Guildhall *Exhibition of Flemish Painting,* London, 1906, No. 3.
1921	Offered for sale on behalf of Mr. C. J. Weld Blundell by Captain Langdon Douglas and acquired by the Felton Bequest in 1922 on the advice of Mr. *Frank Rinder.*
1922	Exhibited at the London National Gallery 16th October-30th December, 1922.
1923	Arrived at Melbourne February 1923.
1939	Exhibited at the New York World Fair 1939, [52] No. 113.
	Exhibited at the Detroit Institute of Arts, Michigan, 1939, [53] No. 12.
1939-40	*Seven Centuries of Painting,* San Francisco, California, [54] No. L-15.

1940   Exhibited at the Cleveland Museum, Ohio, [55] No. 12.

1941   Exhibited at the Cincinnati Art Museum, Ohio, [56] No. 17.

1946   Came back to Melbourne.

1956   Exhibited London National Gallery, November-December, Room XX.

1956   Exhibited at *L'Art Flamand dans les Collections Britanniques*, Bruges, 1956, [66] No. 2.

1960   Returned to Melbourne.

b. *Records of Condition and Treatment*

1850   Described by *Waagen* as having many cracks in 1850 ([3] 249).

1863   *Crowe* and *Cavalcaselle* ([5] 122): except for heavy crackelure, in good preservation.

1883   *Stevenson* ([8] 440) described it as liberally covered with varnish which had darkened and cracked in innumerable lines.

1883   *Weale* ([9] 193) described condition as perfect, without restauration or retouches, despite numerous cracks, caused by the warping of the panel.

1893   *Tschudi* ([12] 101) was the first to mention re-paints when he wrote "not very good condition, numerous disturbing cracks, re-paints and an opaque English varnish".

1901   *Bode* ([18] 122) stated that the picture showed "starke und rohe ältere Übermalung".

1906   *Friedländer* ([24] 574) commented on the unusually heavy opaque varnish and added "und ist vielfach durch alte Retuschen entstellt".

1906   *Weale* ([27] 185) said the picture does not show to full advantage owing to the panel being slightly warped; "this had led to a general crackling of the thick coat of varnish".

1920–21 Mr. *Martin Davies* kindly brought to my attention a letter in the London *Daily Telegraph* in which Mr. *Georg Frederick Zink* ([41] 4) wrote that he had cleaned the *Ince Hall Madonna* and regarded the inscription as genuine. *Friedländer* ([44] 53 f.) stated that *Zink* had cleaned the picture prior to sale to Melbourne. According to a letter from *Frank Rinder*, Felton Adviser to Melbourne, dated June 1922, *Zink* rectified the warping of the panel alluded to by *Weale* ([9]). *Rinder* further stated that Mr. *W. A. Holder* examined the picture.

1957–58 The picture was examined at the Institut royal du Patrimoine artistique in Brussels under Dr. *Paul Coremans*, Messrs. *A. Philippot*, *R. V. Sneyers* and *J. Thissen* in collaboration with Messrs. *Martin Davies*, *F. I. G. Rawlins*, *M. Hey* and Miss *R. J. Plesters* of the London National Gallery. Messrs. *Philippot* and *Sneyers* have summarized the findings under Section C. *Physical Characteristics*. For an extract of Mr. *Davies'* report see Section I, *doc.* 1. The examiners came to the conclusion that the picture is not by Jan van Eyck or any other master of the Flemish 15th century but must be regarded as a copy by a non-flemish artist or a later imitation.

After the examination at Brussels slight paint losses visible in Pl. LI were restored and the bench which is indicated clearly on the left of the cloth of honour and less certainly on the right, has there been strengthened by the restorer, Mr. *A. Philippot*.

In reproductions of the *Ince Hall Madonna* published before 1921 there are only two oranges on the window sill. In *Friedländer* [44] pl. XX a drinking glass appears presumably having been added during *Zink*'s restoration prior to sale to Melbourne (see E. 2 a). In 1958 the glass disappeared in the first stages of cleaning (Pl. LIV b).

F. COMPARATIVE MATERIAL

I. *The whole composition*

Two paintings closely approximating the style and composition of No. 132 are known.

(1) *The Madonna and Child*, private Collection, Rome; in the second half of the nineteenth century in a private collection in Messina, from where it was bought by the Duke of Verdura, Palermo; Duke of Verdura sale, Rome 9-19 April, 1894, Domenico Corvisieri, No. 474; bought by the sister of the Duke, and taken to Palermo; passed by marriage to Baron Paino, Palermo, who sold it between 1925-30 to Baron de Gemmis, Bari, Rome. Now in the possession of his daughter (Pl. LXVI; *Carandente* [80] 46-47, pl. XXII).

First seen by *Bode* before 1892 (*Burlington Fine Arts Club. Exhibition of Pictures by Masters of the Netherlandish and allied Schools of XVth and early XVIth Centuries*, London, 1892, 9, No. 14 a) who described it as a copy of the *Ince Hall Madonna*. Subsequent literature has been compiled by *Carandente, loc. cit.*, who photographed the painting and reproduced it for the first time. He also reports on two labels on the back often referred to in the literature: 1. a label repeating an inscription on the reverse of the panel, referring to a pledge of 1619; this label, transcribed first by *Weale*, 1908 ([30] 67) has subsequently often been said to be on the back of No. 132 thus *Friedländer* ([44] 54). 2. The second label contains a transcript of the two inscriptions on the front, which according to *Carandente* are identical with those in Melbourne. In the reproduction of the front of the Verdura version on Pl. LXVI and on Pl. XXII of *Carandente*'s book the inscriptions remain invisible.

Dated by *Bode* ([18] 122, note 1) 15th century; *von Tschudi* ([13] 244) as from the end of the 15th century; *Carandente* ([80] 47) describes the work as painted on oak, with traces of barbe on all four sides; 36,8×27,7 cm. See also *Author's Comments*, p. 39.

I am indebted to Mr. *Davies* for the analysis of differences between the *Verdura version* and the *Ince Hall picture*: The distance between the head of the Madonna and the baldachin is shorter than in No. 132. The pattern of the stained lead glass that reflects on the reveal is not the same as in Melbourne but more subdivided. The window is less sharply foreshortened; there is more to be seen of it but the view does seem to be against a shutter, not out into the open. It appears that the last leg (near the back wall) of the table on the l. has a formation which has given rise to the Melbourne copyist's continuation of the bench parallel with the backwall. The glass vessel is perhaps smaller, in any case considerably lower down than in Melbourne. The ewer is shown complete. The chest on the right has a horizontal key in the lock and only little knobs on the front, not hinges. The brocade hanging, in relation to the figures is broader; the little pearl bandeau in the hair of the Madonna is not covered by upswept hair at the side, but visible; the folds of her garment remain in front within the horizontal border of the carpet and do not cut across it as in No. 132. As far as one can judge, the quality of the handling, particularly in the jewelry of the Madonna is poor but the faces are more 'Eyckian'. It appears not to be a copy of the Melbourne picture but to pre-suppose the existence of a third picture.

(2) Another replica of the *Madonna and Child* was seen by *Bode* before 1901 in the Museum of Catania which he described as a "wesentlich geringere Kopie, anscheind eine sizilianische Arbeit vom Anfang des XVI. Jahrhunderts" ([18] 122, note 1). See also *Weale* ([30] 67), *Weale* and *Brockwell* ([32] 111), *Friedländer* ([44] 54). This painting is referred to, so Mr. *Davies* kindly informs me, in notes on the back and front of the mount of a photograph of the *Verdura version* in the Victoria and Albert Museum; it is there described as a 19th century copy of the *Verdura version* and as No. 36 of the Catania Museum. *Carandente* states that the picture has disappeared, but suggests that it might be identical with or reflected in the *Pappalardo Madonna and Child* in Catania, *Carandente* [80] pl. XXIII b.

The following versions are more distantly related to the foregoing:

(3) *Madonna and Child in a Room*, Collegiate Church, Covarrubias (Burgos) (Pl. LXVIII a), by a South German Master possibly operating in Spain, *Bruyn* ([67] 123, fig. 51); here the Madonna and Child, the presence of a baldachin and cloth of honour in a domestic interior, the square window openings with lead light above and a short sill in the corner below, the bench underneath the windows, the shadows on the reveal, the candlestick and glass vessels, the presence of inscriptions on the wall appear related to No. 132. *Bruyn* ([67] 123, note 1) rejects *Reinach*'s ([43] 15-16), *Winkler*'s ([49] 258) and *Post*'s ([50] 18-20) assumption that this is a copy of a lost Jan van Eyck, since all its details can be traced back to existing works by Jan or by the Master of Flémalle. *Baldass* ([60] 277, No. 7) calls it an "amplified copy" (of the Melbourne Madonna) "with altered details". See also *Hulin de Loo* (*Un portraitiste de style eyckesque vers 1440*, in *Apollo*, Brussels, December 1951, 8), *Panofsky* ([61] I, 440-441), *Duverger* ([63] 102-104). The picture is wrongly described as by Petrus Christus, signed and dated 1452 in *C. Aru* and *Et. de Geradon, La Galerie Sabauda de Turin* (*Les Primitifs Flamands*, I. *Corpus de la Peinture des anciens Pays-Bas méridionaux au quinzième siècle*, 5), Antwerp, 1952, 4.

(4) Rogier van der Weyden *Madonna Durán*, Madrid, Prado. *Panofsky* ([61] I, 259, II, fig. 317) described this Madonna as manifestly derived from Jan van Eyck's *Ince Hall Madonna*. The red mantle, the inclination of the Madonna's head, the motif of the book, the S curve of the figure are comparable.

(5) *The Madonna and Child in an Interior*, Turin, Gallery Sabauda. *C. Aru* and *Et. de Geradon, loc. cit.*, 1 ff., pl. I-VIII (No. 16, Group Christus) described as Petrus Christus (?). It is doubtful here, whether this is a free variation on the theme of No. 132 or reflecting an independent work, embellished according to *Panofsky* ([61] I, 203, note 5, 440-441) with Flémallian detail. The attitude of the Child, the inclined head of the Madonna may be compared with the Melbourne picture.

(6) Further removed is a *Madonna and Child* by a follower of Jan van Eyck, possibly not Flemish, late 15th century (formerly Coll. Mrs. Simpson Carson); *Bruyn* ([67] 122, fig. 53) suggests that it shows reminiscences of the Melbourne Madonna. The Virgin sits in a domestic interior but the only feature remotely similar is the nature of support of the bench under the window.

II. *Details*

The fruit on the window sill is to be seen in the *Arnolfini Portrait* (*Davies* [62] 122) and in the Frankfurt *Madonna* (*Panofsky* [61] II, fig. 252). The pricket chandelier with two sconce branches occurs in the *Birth of S. John*, Turin Hours (*Panofsky* [61] II, fig. 299); a jug of comparable shape (with spout) appears in Rogier van der Weyden's *Birth and Naming of S. John*, S. John's altarpiece, Berlin (*Panofsky* [61] II, fig. 346), dated by *Panofsky* between 1452 and 55 (*ibid.* 282). The bench (or table) underneath the window has supports similar to those of what is obviously a bench in a *Madonna and Child* by Petrus Christus, at Kansas City (*The Art Quarterly*, Detroit, XX, 1957, 112, repr.). See also No. (6). A similarly short window sill occurs in the *Birth of S. John*, Turin Hours (*Panofsky* [61] II, fig. 299) and elsewhere. Chest and table in this miniature may be compared with the chest or cupboard on the right in No. 132. A similar basin is frequent, cf. for example the Frankfurt *Madonna* (*Panofsky* [61] II, fig. 252). I have not come across a glass carafe of comparable shape in any of the Flemish paintings of the 15th century; that vessels of this shape existed however is born out by fig. 35 of a bottle dated about 1500, Worms Museum, in *J. Schlosser, Das Alte Glas*, Brunswick, 1956.

G. AUTHOR'S COMMENTS

The attribution of the *Madonna and Child* to Jan van Eyck, general until 1958, cannot be upheld. The account under C. *Physical Characteristics*, convincingly shows that the technique of No. 132 is un-Eyckian and un-Flemish, on account of abnormalities of the structure and composition of the paint layer, the unusual pattern of cracks, the absence of unpainted edges and of barbe, to mention only some of the relevant features discussed under C. In particular the building up of the structure of the face and hands of the Madonna and of the Child with lead white is inconsistent with van Eyck's method; as has been pointed out by *Erwin Panofsky*, Jan van Eyck used white lead sparingly (letter to *Eric Westbrook*, 24 Feb. 1959). The poor draughtsmanship of the white lead passages is illustrated in the comparison between Pl. L (X-ray of *Ince Hall Madonna*) and Pl. LXVII (*Holy Maidens*, Ghent). The lack of quality and precision in the handling, the errors in the construction of the cupboard (Section I, *doc. 1, Davies*), the meaningless pentimenti in the window frame (*ibid.*) have no parallel in Jan van Eyck's œuvre. The clumsy and faulty inscription (*ibid.*) having proved to be contemporaneous with the main paint layer further weakens the case for authenticity of the *Ince Hall Madonna*.

Subject to certain restrictions mentioned by *Davies, ibid.*, No. 132 may be taken to reflect more or less faithfully a lost original by Jan van Eyck. The details of furniture, metal work, glass and costume are usual in Flemish 15th century paintings (see F. *Comparative Material*, II). Several other versions and variations of the composition and echoes of the Child with Book (F. *Comparative Material*, I and D. *Description and Iconography*) show that the original of No. 132 enjoyed a distinct popularity between 1437 and the early 16th century. It seems therefore possible to assume that the *Ince Hall Madonna* also originated during this period.

The question has been raised whether the inscription was placed on the back wall of the original by Jan van Eyck or by another painter, who copied it from the original frame, the usual place for van Eyck signatures. Instances of Flemish 15th century signatures occurring within the pictorial space have been cited: *Davies* (Doc. 1) drew attention to the *Arnolfini Wedding* by Jan van Eyck and a miniature by Loiset Liédet. *Levey* ([74] 125) mentions the *Timothy* by Jan van Eyck. No instances of an inscription copied later on to the front of the panel from a frame is known to me.

The unusual inclusion of *Brugis* in the signature allows me to speculate whether the wording of the inscription was varied by a non-Flemish painter. The Examiners of the Institut royal du Patrimoine artistique, while disclaiming the Flemish origin of the *Madonna and Child* do not exclude the possibility that it was done elsewhere at an early date by an artist unfamiliar with Flemish technique. It might be thought that the picture was of Sicilian origin, since two other versions of the composition have been known since the nineteenth century to exist in Sicilian collections. Here it must be stated first, that the *Verdura version* (F. *Comparative Material*, I, 1) is not a copy of the *Ince Hall Madonna*, as assumed by *Bode, Friedländer* and others, but must be based on a common original (I, *doc. 1, Davies*). The *Catania version* (F. *Comparative Material*, I, 2) is now lost. Its relation to the other two versions is obscure; if one were to agree with *Carandente* ([80] 47-48) who suggests that the picture *Bode* saw in 1901 in the Museum of Catania may be identical with, or reflected in, the *Madonna and Child in a Landscape* now in the Pappalardo Collection ([80] pl. XXIII b), the similarities between this picture and the other versions is so slight, that it is impossible to say whether it was inspired by a common original or by the *Verdura copy* itself. The argument for a Sicilian origin of No. 132 is further weakened by the fact that the *Verdura copy* itself is not by a Sicilian hand. *Carandente* describes it as painted on oak with remnants of 'barbe', that is, as the work of a Flemish painter. Its Sicilian provenance can only be traced with certainty to the middle of the nineteenth century. Should one assume that the original by van Eyck from which the *Verdura copy* was taken was in Sicily at an early date, one would have to assume also the presence of a Flemish painter there in the late 15th or early 16th century. No other work of such a painter is known. The circumstances surrounding the Sicilian versions of the *Ince Hall Madonna* therefore lend little support to the assumption of a Sicilian origin of this work and less to an assumption of Sicilian workmanship.

If it is assumed with *Bruyn* ([67] 123) that the *Madonna and Child* at Covarrubias, executed by a South German Master possibly active in Spain, reflects a knowledge of the original of the *Ince Hall Madonna*, the latter might be thought to be of Spanish origin. (For the assumption that this South German Master worked in Bruges, see *Hulin de Loo*, in *Apollo*, December 1941, 8). No supporting evidence for a Spanish origin of No. 132 is at present available.

The history of the Blundell Collection, much of which appears to have been bought in Italy, may suggest an Italian origin of the picture, but no clear information on the circumstances and date of entry of this picture into the Blundell collection is available. On the information available at present, it is not possible for me to come to a conclusion in this matter and the problem must be left for future research.

As *Held* pointed out ([64] 217) the poor lettering of the inscription makes it permissible to doubt the accuracy of its contents. Was 1433 the date of the original? As stated above, E. 1.b, *Pächt* ([65] 274, note 32) and *Grossmann* ([68] 3-4) suggest an earlier date as more in keeping with the Flémallian simplicity of the Madonna's garment and the gothic S curve of her position. *Baldass* ([60] 51), without actually suggesting an earlier date, stressed the similarity of the way in which the figure is hidden by folds, and performs an S curve, to the Berlin *Madonna* (No. 525 c) usually dated before 1430. *Tolnay* ([51] 25) by implication dated the comparable *Madonna at the Fireplace* (Leningrad) ascribed to Robert Campin earlier than the *Ince Hall Madonna*. *Panofsky* ([61] I, 173) however, dated the *Campin Madonna* later. The authors of the *Corpus Leningrad* ([77] 17) date the Campin ca. 1433-35. The *Leningrad Madonna* therefore offers no clear support for the dating of the original of No. 132.

Since the earliest echo of the Child with book occurs in Rogier van der Weyden's *Durán Madonna* (Madrid) of 1437, and the domestic interior bears a certain resemblance to Jan van Eyck's *Arnolfini Wedding* (London) of 1434, I feel that 1433 remains a likely date for the original of the *Ince Hall Madonna*.

U. H.

L'examen et le nettoyage de la Madone d'Ince Hall ont révélé des divergences profondes entre ce tableau et les œuvres flamandes du XVᵉ siècle. Du point de vue composition et structure matérielles ces divergences affectent non pas des détails isolés mais l'ensemble de l'œuvre. Le graphique est également de qualité nettement inférieure à celle de van Eyck et des grands Primitifs flamands. Il n'est donc pas possible d'incorporer ce tableau dans l'œuvre eyckienne ou dans celle d'un autre maître flamand du XVᵉ siècle et il faut bien admettre qu'il s'agit d'une copie ou d'une imitation tardive.

L'interprétation la plus favorable peut reconnaître un tableau ancien composé sur le type eyckien à l'instar d'autres versions mentionnées dans la littérature. Peut-être faut-il alors y adjoindre la restriction que la méconnaissance des principes picturaux restés si longtemps en honneur dans les Flandres fait songer à un peintre non flamand.

L'hypothèse que l'œuvre daterait d'une période plus récente n'est cependant pas exclue du point de vue technique. Cette hypothèse marque une réelle discordance avec les données historiques. Le problème reste ouvert et sa solution exige encore l'apport d'informations complémentaires, tant sur le plan de la technique que sur celui de l'histoire.

A. P. and R. V. S.

H. BIBLIOGRAPHY

1803 [1] : *An Account of the Paintings at Ince*, collected by H. B., date 1803, photostat National Gallery, London.

1853 [2] : E. FÖRSTER, *Geschichte der deutschen Kunst*, II, Leipzig, 1853.

1854 [3] : [G. F.] WAAGEN, *Treasures of Art in Great Britain*, III, London, 1854.

1862 [4] : G. F. WAAGEN, *Handbuch der deutschen und niederländischen Malerschulen*, Stuttgart, 1862.

1863 [5] : J. A. CROWE and G. B. CAVALCASELLE, *Les anciens peintres flamands. Leur vie et leurs œuvres [...]. Annoté et augmenté de documents inédits* par A. PINCHART et CH. RUELENS, II, Brussels, 1863.

1866 [6] : ALFRED MICHIELS, *Histoire de la Peinture flamande depuis ses débuts jusqu'en 1864*, 2nd ed., II, Paris, 1866.

1879 [7] : CARL SCHNAASE and O. EISENMANN, *Geschichte der bildenden Künste im 15. Jahrhundert*, VIII, Stuttgart, 1879.

1883 [8] : [R. A. M. STEVENSON], *The private Collections of England. No. LXXVI–Ince Blundell Hall, Liverpool*, in *The Athenaeum* (London), Oct. 6, 1883, 439-440.

1883 [9] : W. H. JAMES WEALE, *Les trésors de l'art chrétien en Angleterre*, in *Revue de l'art chrétien* (Lille/Bruges), 3rd ser., Vol. I, 1883, 62-66 and 193-195.

1884 [10] : CLAUDE PHILLIPS, *Exposition d'hiver à l'Académie des Beaux-Arts de Londres*, in *Gazette des Beaux-Arts* (Paris), 2nd ser., Vol. XXIX, 1884, 181.

1892 [11] : PAUL LEPRIEUR, *Correspondance d'Angleterre*, in *Gazette des Beaux-Arts* (Paris), 3rd ser., Vol. VIII, 1892, 170.

1893 [12] : HUGO VON TSCHUDI, *London. Die Ausstellung altniederländischer Gemälde im Burlington Fine Arts Club*, in *Repertorium für Kunstwissenschaft* (Berlin/Stuttgart), Vol. XVI, 1893, 100-116.

1894 [13] : [HUGO] V[ON] T[SCHUDI], *Versteigerung der Sammlung des Herzogs von Verdura*, in *Repertorium für Kunstwissenschaft* (Berlin/Stuttgart), Vol. XVII, 1894, 244.

1898 [14] : LUDWIG KAEMMERER, *Hubert und Jan van Eyck*, Bielefeld/Leipzig, 1898.

1899 [15] : OTTO SEECK, *Die charakteristischen Unterschiede der Brüder van Eyck*, Extract from *Abhandlungen der Königlichen Gesellschaft der Wissenschaften zu Göttingen*, N.S., Vol. III, 1, Berlin, 1899, 70.

1900 [16] : KARL VOLL, *Die Werke des Jan van Eyck. Eine kritische Studie*, Strassburg, 1900.

1900 [17] : [MAX J.] FRIEDLÄNDER, *Litteraturbericht. Karl Voll, Die Werke des Jan van Eyck*, in *Repertorium für Kunstwissenschaft* (Berlin), Vol. XXIII, 1900, 470-479.

1901 [18] : WILHELM BODE, *Jan van Eycks Bildnis eines burgundischen Kammerherrn*, in *Jahrbuch der Königlich Preussischen Kunstsammlungen* (Berlin), Vol. XXII, 1901, 115-131.

1901 [19] : LUDWIG KAEMMERER, *Die Neueste Eycklitteratur*, in *Kunstchronik* (Leipzig), N.F. XII, No. 5, 1901, 65-74.

1904 [20] :   G. JOSEPH KERN, *Die Grundzüge der linear-perspektivischen Darstellungen in der Kunst der Gebrüder van Eyck und ihrer Schule*, Leipzig, 1904.

1905 [21] :   E. DURAND-GRÉVILLE, *Hubert van Eyck, son œuvre et son influence*, I, in *Les Arts anciens de Flandre* (Bruges), Vol. I, 1905, 11-36.

1905 [22] :   FIERENS-GEVAERT, *Etudes sur l'art flamand. La Renaissance septentrionale et les premiers maîtres des Flandres*, Brussels, 1905.

1906 [23] :   DANIEL BURCKHARDT, *Studien zur Geschichte der Altoberrheinischen Malerei*, in *Jahrbuch der Königlich Preuszischen Kunstsammlungen* (Berlin), Vol. XXVII, 1906, 179-197.

1906 [24] :   [MAX J.] FRIEDLÄNDER, *Die Leihausstellung in der Guildhall zu London*, in *Repertorium für Kunstwissenschaft* (Berlin), Vol. XXIX, 1906, 573-582.

1906 [25] :   MARGARETE SIEBERT, *Die Madonnendarstellung in der Altniederländischen Kunst von Jan van Eyck bis zu den Manieristen*, Strassburg, 1906.

1906 [26] :   KARL VOLL, *Die Altniederländische Malerei von Jan van Eyck bis Memling*, Leipzig, 1906.

1906 [27] :   W. H. JAMES WEALE, *Netherlandish Art at the Guildhall*, I, in *The Burlington Magazine* (London), Vol. IX, 1906, 184-194.

1906 [28] :   ALFRED VON WURZBACH, *Eyck. Jan (...)*, in *Niederländisches Künstler-Lexikon*, I, Vienna/Leipzig, 1906, 509-521.

1907 [29] :   CLAUDE PHILLIPS, *A "Crucifixion", by Konrad Witz of Basel*, in *The Burlington Magazine* (London), Vol. XI, 1907, 103-109.

1908 [30] :   W. H. JAMES WEALE, *Hubert and John van Eyck, Their Life and Work*, London/New York, 1908.

1911 [31] :   ERIC MACLAGAN, *Letter to the Editors. "Hubert and John van Eyck"*, in *The Burlington Magazine* (London), Vol. XIX, 1911, 242.

1912 [32] :   W. H. JAMES WEALE and MAURICE W. BROCKWELL, *The Van Eycks and their Art*, London/New York/Toronto, 1912.

1914 [33] :   HERMANN FÜRBRINGER, *Die künstlerischen Voraussetzungen des Genter Altars der Brüder van Eyck*, Inaugural-Dissertation, Weida i. Th., 1914.

1915 [34] :   MAX J. FRIEDLÄNDER, *Eyck, Jan van*, in *Allgemeines Lexikon der bildenden Künstler von der Antike bis zur Gegenwart* (begründet von U. THIEME und F. BECKER), Leipzig, XI, 1915, 129-133.

1916 [35] :   MAX J. FRIEDLÄNDER, *Von Eyck bis Bruegel*, Berlin, 1916.

1921 [36] :   MARTIN CONWAY, *The Van Eycks and their Followers*, London, 1921.

1921 [37] :   MAX J. FRIEDLÄNDER, *Von Eyck bis Bruegel*, Berlin, 1921.

1922 [38] :   CHARLES J. HOLMES, *A Van Eyck for Melbourne*, in *The Burlington Magazine* (London), Vol. XLI, 1922, 232, 235.

1922 [39] :   KURT PFISTER, *Van Eyck*, Munich, 1922.

1922 [40] :   CLAUDE PHILLIPS, *A Jan van Eyck for Melbourne*, in *The Daily Telegraph* (London), October 14, 1922, 13.

1922 [41] :   GEORG FREDERICK ZINK, letter in *The Daily Telegraph* (London), October 17, 1922, 4.

1923 [42] :   MAURICE W. BROCKWELL, *The Ince-Blundell van Eyck*, in *Art in America* (New York), Vol. XI, 1923, 143-149.

1923 [43] :   SALOMON REINACH, *A Copy from a lost van Eyck*, in *The Burlington Magazine* (London), Vol. XLIII, 1923, 14-16.

1924 [44] :   MAX J. FRIEDLÄNDER, *Die Altniederländische Malerei*, I. *Die van Eyck. Petrus Christus*, Berlin, 1924.

1924 [45] : AUGUST SCHMARSOW, *Hubert und Jan van Eyck*, Leipzig, 1924.

1924 [46] : HANS WENDLAND, *Konrad Witz. Gemäldestudien*, Basel, 1924.

1926 [47] : MARGUERITE DEVIGNE, *Van Eyck*, Brussels/Paris, 1926.

1930 [48] : MAX J. FRIEDLÄNDER, in W. R. VALENTINER, *Chefs-d'œuvre inconnus des grands maîtres*, I, Paris/Brussels, 1930.

1931 [49] : FRIEDRICH WINKLER, *Die Stifter des Lebensbrunnens und andere van Eyck-Fragen*, II, in *Pantheon* (Munich), Vol. VII, 1931, 255-259.

1933 [50] : CHANDLER RATHFON POST, *A History of Spanish Painting*, Cambridge, Mass., IV, Part I, 1933.

1939 [51] : CHARLES DE TOLNAY, *Le Maître de Flémalle et les Frères van Eyck*, Brussels, 1939.

1939 [52] : WILLIAM R. VALENTINER, GEORGE HENRY McCALL, *Catalogue of European Paintings and Sculpture from 1300-1800*, New York World's Fair, New York, May-October 1939.

1939 [53] : *Masterpieces of Art from Foreign Collections. European Paintings from the two World's Fairs. The Detroit Institute of Art*, November 10 through December 10, 1939.

1939 [54] : *Seven Centuries of Painting. A Loan Exhibition of Old and Modern Masters. The California Palace of the Legion of Honor and the M.H. de Young Memorial Museum. San Francisco*, December 29, 1939 to January 28, 1940.

1940 [55] : *Masterpieces of Art from the New York and San Francisco World's Fairs, The Cleveland Museum of Art* February 7 through March 7, 1940.

1941 [56] : *Masterpieces of Art: European Paintings from the New York and San Francisco World's Fair (...) Cincinnati Art Museum*, January 15 through February 9, 1941.

1943 [57] : HERMANN BEENKEN, *Hubert und Jan van Eyck*, 2nd ed., Munich, 1943.

1947 [58] : H. A. SCHMID, *Witz, Konrad*, in *Allgemeines Lexikon der bildenden Künstler von der Antike bis zur Gegenwart* (begründet von U. THIEME und F. BECKER, herausgegeben von H. VOLLMER), Leipzig, XXXVI, 1947, 148-155.

1948 [59] : THEODOR MUSPER, *Untersuchungen zu Rogier van der Weyden und Jan van Eyck*, Stuttgart, (1948).

1952 [60] : LUDWIG BALDASS, *Jan van Eyck*, (London, 1952).

1953 [61] : ERWIN PANOFSKY, *Early Netherlandish Painting, Its Origins and Character*, Cambridge, Mass., 1953, 2 vols.

1954 [62] : MARTIN DAVIES, *The National Gallery, London* (*Les Primitifs flamands, I. Corpus de la Peinture des anciens Pays-Bas méridionaux au quinzième siècle*, 3), II, Antwerp, 1954.

1955 [63] : J. DUVERGER, *Brugse Schilders ten tijde van Jan van Eyck*, in *Bulletin des Musées Royaux des Beaux-Arts* (Brussels), 1-3, 1955, 83-120.

1955 [64] : JULIUS HELD, review of Erwin Panofsky, *Early Netherlandish Painting, Its Origins and Character*, Cambridge (Mass.), *1953*, in *The Art Bulletin* (New York), Vol. XXXVII, 1955, 205-234.

1956 [65] : OTTO PÄCHT, *Panofsky's "Early Netherlandish Painting"*, II, in *The Burlington Magazine* (London), Vol. XCVIII, 1956, 266-279.

1956 [66] : *L'Art flamand dans les Collections Britanniques. Musée Communal Groeninge - Bruges*, August-September 1956, Brussels, 1956.

1957 [67] : JOSUA BRUYN, *Van Eyck Problemen*, Utrecht, 1957.

1957 [68] : F. GROSSMANN, *Flemish Paintings at Bruges*, in *The Burlington Magazine* (London), Vol. XCIX, 1957, 2-9.

1959 [69] : NP., *Ein unechter Van Eyck?*, in *Die Weltkunst* (Munich), Vol. 29, 1959, No. 23, 18.

1960 [70] : JOHN JACOB, *Catalogue of the Pictures at Ince Blundell Hall, Walker Art Gallery*, Liverpool, April 3-31, 1960.

1961 [71] : VALENTIN DENIS, *All the Paintings of Jan van Eyck*, London, 1961.

1961 [72] : URSULA HOFF, *Catalogue of European Paintings before Eighteen-Hundred. National Gallery of Victoria*, Melbourne, 1961.

1961 [73] : MILLARD MEISS, *"Highlands" in the Lowlands. Jan van Eyck, the Master of Flémalle and the Franco-Italian Tradition*, in *Gazette des Beaux-Arts* (Paris/New York), 6th ser., Vol. LVII, 1961, 273-314.

1962 [74] : MICHAEL LEVEY, review of *National Gallery of Victoria, Melbourne: Catalogue of European Painting (...)*, in *Museums Journal* (London), Vol. 62, No. 2, 1962, 124-126.

1962 [75] : KEITH ROBERTS, review of *Valentin Denis, All the Paintings by Jan van Eyck, London 1962*, in *The Connoisseur* (London), Vol. 151, 1962, 51-52.

1963 [76] : JACQUELINE FOLIE, *Les œuvres authentifiées des Primitifs flamands*, in *Bulletin de l'Institut royal du Patrimoine artistique* (Brussels), Vol. VI, 1963, 183-256.

1965 [77] : VLADIMIR LOEWINSON-LESSING and NICOLAS NICOULINE, *Le Musée de l'Ermitage. Leningrad* (*Les Primitifs flamands*, I. *Corpus de la Peinture des anciens Pays-Bas méridionaux au quinzième siècle*, 8), Brussels, 1965.

1967 [78] : MAX J. FRIEDLÄNDER, *Early Netherlandish Painting*, I. *The van Eycks. Petrus Christus*, Leyden/Brussels, 1967.

1967 [79] : URSULA HOFF, *Catalogue of European Paintings before Eighteen Hundred. National Gallery of Victoria*, 2nd, enlarged ed., Melbourne, 1967.

1968 [80] : GIOVANNI CARANDENTE, *Collections d'Italie*, I. *Sicile* (*Les Primitifs flamands*, II. *Répertoire des Peintures flamandes du quinzième siècle*, 3), Brussels, 1968.

I. TRANSCRIPTIONS OF DOCUMENTS AND LITERARY SOURCES

1.

London, 12 November, 1958.
Report from Mr. Martin Davies, *director of the London National Gallery.*

THE INCE BLUNDELL MADONNA AT MELBOURNE

This report is supplementary to the technical report from Brussels, and merely refers from time to time to a selection of the technical data.

In the compte-rendu from the Brussels Laboratory, dated 14 May 1958, it is stated that various details of the picture after cleaning have been tested; evidence has not been found that these details, most of which will be referred to in the present report, are distortingly retouched. It might indeed be expected that paint in cracks or over losses is later repair; this view is admitted as possible, in the present case as normally, in the report from Brussels, but it is there not excluded either that such paint may be the completion of the original picture by the original painter. My criticisms in this report of various details are criticisms of what I have seen, in particular on 26 April 1958. How likely is it that what was then to be seen differs substantially from the original state of the picture? The technical evidence is given in the (compte-rendu and) report from Brussels; I wish to record that, in my view, the likelihood is little.

The Signature on the Melbourne Picture.

Since this picture bears an inscription to the effect that it was painted by Jan van Eyck, the attribution cannot be doubted unless the inscription is in some way doubted too. It should therefore be discussed first; everything I think suitable for comment in this report about the inscription will be dealt with now.

As is well known, this inscription has sometimes been said not to be Jan van Eyck's work.

It should be stated first that its position on the back wall, although that may be thought strange, is no proof that Jan van Eyck did not put it there. The position of the signature on his Arnolfini picture in London settles that. The case of another painter who placed his signature on a wall may be cited, the miniaturist Loyset Liedet; see J. van den Gheyn, *Histoire de Charles Martel*, 1910, Plate 92.

The signature itself, nevertheless, seems to me unworthy of Jan van Eyck. Inscriptions by him are found on several pictures; it seems to me that the poor lettering excludes Jan van Eyck's work in this case.

In support of this judgment, I specify various peculiarities; these, or some of them, should shake belief that the inscription was written by Jan van Eyck.

(a) The last letter of the second word of the motto should be an H; it does not seem to resemble the remains of what must be an H, in IOHEM, on the left. It does resemble quite closely the letter A, occurring elsewhere in this inscription; and there is a presumption that the writer here of Als ixh xan did not understand what he was writing.

(b) The spelling of the name as EYC is very strange; I do not know that Jan van Eyck spelt his name in this way. It is true that some marks on tiles in the Ghent altarpiece have been read as *v(an) Eyc*, and claimed as perhaps signatures (J. de Borchgrave d'Altena, *Le Polyptyque de l'Agneau est-il signé?*, 1941).

(c) The form $\overline{\text{ANO}}$ D instead of $\overline{\text{ANO}}$ $\overline{\text{DNI}}$ or $\overline{\text{ANO}}$ D^{I} seems to me strange.

(d) To begin the word $\text{COPLET}\overline{\text{V}}$ without the usual abbreviation for *con* or *com* (?) seems to be unusual in Jan van Eyck's work. Here, however, the inscription on the frame of the Dresden Triptych may be cited, where the beginning of the work *comparata* must be read as the three letters *com*.

The photograph of the Verdura version shows that peculiarity (d) there corresponds; (a) may correspond, but I cannot see for certain; the matter of (c) is more doubtful still; I cannot see at all for (b).

It may be thought that peculiarities (b) and (c) at Melbourne are due to lack of space, the edge of the hanging being an obvious bar to an extension of the inscription. I think that this may well be so. Indeed, it might be held that the ends of these two lines of the inscription already pass over on to the front of the hanging, absurd as that is; and the fact that the date is not quite easy to read correctly may seem a third example of the writer's not having allowed enough space. If this is so, I think that on that ground Jan van Eyck should not be credited with having written the inscription; he would, I think, have allowed sufficient space.

If the inscription was not written by Jan van Eyck, it may yet be thought to have been copied from an inscription by him, now missing but originally associated with the picture. No trace of another inscription on the back wall has been found. It has been suggested that the original inscription may have been on the missing original frame. But the Brussels Laboratory has not found evidence that the paint of the present inscription is less authentic than the rest of the picture. It should also be recalled that the Verdura version carries an inscription in the same place, although this point would seem at best only moderately strong and is weakened, I think, by the difference already noted between the two inscriptions.

My opinions are: (1) that the inscription we see was not written by Jan van Eyck; and (2) that the inscription we see is coeval with the picture, and in particular was not copied later from the frame or elsewhere. If both these opinions are admitted to be true, the picture could hardly be considered a work by Jan van Eyck, and further discussion might be dispensed with. If it is felt that the second point, in spite of what has been said, remains doubtful, I would still claim that the arguments in favour of (1) are very strong indeed; if (1) is admitted, the presence of the inscription does not settle the attribution of the picture, on which I will now comment.

Stylistic Comments on the Melbourne Picture.

This picture is either an original Jan van Eyck; or else a copy or an imitation. If it is not an original, the painter is likely to have done his best in the most prominent parts, and it is legitimate to look first, and indeed chiefly, for failings in subsidiary parts. The comments will concern details. It should be stressed that at a casual glance the general effect of the Melbourne picture is quite good; but the pictures by Jan van Eyck not only give a good general effect, but also pass a rigorous examination of details.

(1) The carpet is painted roughly, with dirty-looking colours; this is not like the carpet in the Arnolfini picture, which was on view close by when the Melbourne picture was in London. It is true that the Melbourne picture has since been cleaned at Brussels; but I do not find that the quality of the carpet has changed noticeably. In one case noted, a line of this carpet fails to stop short at the edge of the Virgin's mantle, but extends over it for about 1 mm., such carelessness is not characteristic of Jan van Eyck.

(2) The lock of the cupboard and the keys hanging from it are formless, painted as if rapidly, in a way I think uncharacteristic of Jan van Eyck. The key in the lock is not horizontal, i.e. not properly in; one may even wonder if the executant thought he was painting a piece of ironwork attached to the front – the perspective would suit. The shadow of the bunch of keys seems to be misunderstood; since the bunch stands away from the cupboard, one would expect the shadow to be shown as detached from the bunch.

(3) I am puzzled by the construction of this cupboard. The ironwork on the front at the near end must be, I think, the hinges of a door; if it were merely to strengthen the piece of furniture, it would, I think, grip the corner and not be only on the front. These hinges, then, and indeed the placing of objects on the top of the cupboard, and what is seen of the construction of the near top corner, strongly suggest that there is a door in the front; but then the lock, I think, should be at the side, opposite the hinges. The position of the lock at the top would suit a lid that lifts up. It may be added that at the far end of the front of the cupboard there are marks that at least have not been proved to be retouches by a restorer; they look to me like summary indications of a second set of hinges, which would make the construction even more difficult to accept. The painting of this cupboard is so rough that it is perhaps unwise to try to define what is seen, even as far as I have done. Yet I think I am justified in claiming that the executant did not understand what he was doing when painting it; if that is true, the executant was not Jan van Eyck.

(4) Some rough repairs to holes in the base of the candlestick may be thought contemporary with the painting of the candlestick itself (see the technical report from Brussels, and the compte-rendus dated 21 February and 14 May 1958); I am confident that Jan van Eyck would not have permitted himself repairs such as these.

(5) The bench in front of the window at the left continues against the back wall to the left of the hanging. Is this continuation of the bench found also against the back wall to the right of the hanging? I think it may be, but the indications of it are so vague that even after careful examination I am not sure. I do not think that Jan van Eyck would have left the matter thus.

(6) So far as I can see, there is no difference between the painting of the mullion of the window and the edge of what must be the shutter outside; yet the one ought, I think, to represent stone and the other wood.

(7) In the shadow of the glass leads in the top part of the window, the line of the lower main bar is, in the part next the window itself, not in the right direction. The error may seem slight, but it calls attention to itself, even among the feebly drawn details of this shadow; it is clear in a photograph of the whole picture, although the detail in question is there very small. I think that Jan van Eyck would have avoided this error.

(8) I could not say anything in favour of the execution of the hanging, but limit myself to noting what I think is the most obviously feeble part, the fringe of the baldacchine.

It is difficult to specify comprehensibly what is wrong with the appearance of the more prominent parts. It may suffice if I point out:

(9) that the feebly wavy contours of the Virgin's mantle seem to me foreign to Jan van Eyck's work; the point may demonstrate itself clearly enough if a photograph is looked at upside down. (For technical comment on these contours, see the report from Brussels).

(10) that as seen in an $\times 5$ macrophotograph (before cleaning, but no significant difference noted since the cleaning), the formless right pupil of the Child exudes over the lower eyelid, and His formless left pupil over the upper eyelid. My conviction is that important details on a small scale, when painted by Jan van Eyck, are not seen to be inefficiently done on being magnified five times.

Some of the points noted above may be considered in relation to the Verdura picture, known to me only in an old photograph. I do not see in the Verdura picture the continuation of the bench against the back wall, and this point will be referred to again presently. The lock and keys there seem to be painted rather less carelessly, and the key is better placed in the lock. These points seem not to offer support to the view that the Melbourne picture is an original from which the Verdura picture was copied.

I have examined the parts of the Melbourne picture not commented on above; I have not found any part clearly worthy of Jan van Eyck. Further adverse remarks on the execution will be found in the report from Brussels. In my view, the attribution of the picture to Jan van Eyck is excluded by the quality of the painting.

Copy or Imitation.

If the Melbourne picture is not an original, it may be more or less exactly a copy of some work by Jan van Eyck; alternatively, it could be an imitation of Jan van Eyck's style (or, if preferred, of Eyckish style), some details being presumably based on various originals, but not derived as a whole from any single work by Jan van Eyck. The difficulties in the second view are considerable, and I think that they need not be analysed here unless it is found that the first alternative involves great improbabilities. I note therefore the following unusual points about the Melbourne picture; these may be thought distinct from any stylistic peculiarities already noted, all of which, I think, may be ascribed to the inefficiency or whim of the executant.

(a) The scene is unusually secular for Jan van Eyck. True, some of the still-life may be held to have a symbolical meaning for the religious theme; yet the setting of the picture remains uncharacteristic of this painter. I think that the nearest parallel is the *Virgin and Child* at Frankfort; but that seems to me distinctly less secular. The Verdura picture seems not to differ from the one at Melbourne in this respect; in the picture at Covarrubias, the inclusion of prayer beads puts it less in disaccord with what is known of Jan van Eyck's taste in the matter. (The haloes at Covarrubias are left out of account; they do not suggest Jan van Eyck's style to me).

(b) The Virgin's mantle is plain, here and in the Verdura picture. A comparable example, ascribed to van Eyck, is in the ex-Turin miniature of *The Virgin among Virgins*, and it is true that in some pictures by Jan van Eyck there is a tendency to plainness; yet the mantle at Melbourne seems to me uncharacteristic.

(c) What must be a shutter to the window opens outwards. Normally, shutters opened inwards, though there may in addition be a light second shutter opening outwards. Although the arrangement in the Melbourne picture (and probably in the Verdura version too) appears to be unusual, I know of some other examples, e.g. in the *Annunciation* by the Master of Liesborn (National Gallery, London, No. 256); examples in Netherlandish painting of the first half of the XV century may exist, but I do not know of them.

(d) The arrangement of the bench in front of the window, with its window-shelf or shelves, in the Melbourne, Verdura and Covarrubias pictures, seems to be unusual. It is paralleled more or less in the Turin miniature of *The Birth of S. John;* though there the bench (?) is a seat, which is at least not clearly the case here. A closer parallel is found in the *Virgin and Child* assigned to Petrus Christus, recently acquired for Kansas City. Neither of these offers a parallel for the continuation of the bench against the back wall. This, as already noted, seems not to be included in the Verdura version, nor can I trace it in reproductions of the Covarrubias picture; it is awkwardly contrived, and I think it is awkwardly conceived.

I have sought for peculiarities in the Melbourne picture that might suggest it is not a copy of a Jan van Eyck, but rather an imitation; these are the four I have found worth noting. I doubt if they would suffice to preclude the Melbourne picture from being a copy of a missing Jan van Eyck, even if the copy were assumed to be throughout exact. But I see no necessity for this assumption; indeed, the fact that the Melbourne picture is varied from the Verdura version seems to put the assumption, to say the least, in need of defence. I further call attention to one of the changes in composition I have noticed in the Melbourne picture. It seems clear from the X-ray photograph that the window at the left has been heightened, and that at first part of the extreme top and a piece of the wall above it were shown; this change is hardly in accord with the view that the Melbourne picture is an exact copy of another.

For the purposes of discussion, it has been assumed that the Verdura picture is not an original Jan van Eyck. If it turned out to be so, the section above may simply be cancelled; yet I think that cancellation on this ground should not be confidently expected.

It is, I suppose, legitimate to think that the postulated original was a miniature; but I do not know of evidence to suggest that a picture is not more likely.

SUMMARY

In my view, the Melbourne picture is not an original painting by Jan van Eyck. I think it is a copy, probably not exact but made with some variations; the amount of variation cannot be defined at present, but may be considerable.

As for the date of execution, the technical evidence is not a subject for my comment. Henry Blundell (d. 1810) is indeed the man who formed the Ince Collection. Admittedly, some things were acquired after his time; his successor specified two in his will, a piece of an ornamental tripod and an ancient head of the Indian Bacchus or Jupiter. But such acquisitions are not likely to have been numerous; Henry Blundell bequeathed the larger part of his income to daughters, and thereupon, and again upon the death of his successor, the estate was involved in costly litigation (see T. E. Gibson, *Lydiate Hall and its Associations*, 1876).

I have no evidence for a date more precise than almost certainly before 1810.

A copy may be made with intent to deceive, or else not. I do not think that the presence of the "signature" on the Melbourne picture is a decisive argument in favour of the first alternative. I do not find other argument, for or against, to include in my report; the technical evidence that may bear on this question is stated in the report from Brussels.

(Signed) MARTIN DAVIES
12 November 1958

(*Melbourne, files of the National Gallery of Victoria*).

J. LIST OF PLATES

No. 132: GROUP EYCK (9)

XLIX.	The Madonna and the Child, after restoration	B	175 210	1959
L.	The Madonna and the Child, X-radiograph	B	L 7 301	1958
LI.	The Madonna and the Child, after cleaning and before restoration	B	L 7 333	1958
LII.	The Madonna and the Child, infra-red	B	L 4 434	1956
LIII.	a) The Reverse	B	165 017	1956
	b) The right edge of the planed panel (M 10×)	B	L 6 516	1957
LIV.	a) The left edge, with the groove traced in the paint layer (M 15×)	B	L 7 071	1958
	b) The groove near the left edge and the still-life on the window-sill, after cleaning (M 5×)	B	L 7 067	1958
LV.	Bust of the Virgin and Child (M 2½×)	B	165 020	1956
LVI.	The Child and the still-life on the left (M 2×)	B	165 022	1956
LVII.	The still-life, the cupboard and the right edge (M 2×)	B	165 021	1956
LVIII.	The lower left corner (M 2×)	B	165 025	1956
LIX.	a) Detail showing the folds in the Virgin's mantle (M 5×)	B	L 5 790	1956
	b) Detail showing the wooden floor and the carpet below the Virgin's mantle (M 20×)	B	L 7 227	1958
LX.	The inscription on the left after the removal of the transparent protein film (M 5×)	B	L 7 224	1958
LXI.	The inscription on the right (M 5×)	B	L 5 794	1956
LXII.	Detail showing the face of the Virgin, with touching up or retouching strokes (M 20×)	B	L 7 235	1958
LXIII.	Detail of the left part of the brocade hanging revealing, after cleaning, the transparent protein film (M 20×)	B	L 7 244	1958
LXIV.	a) The Virgin's head (M 5×)	B	L 5 786	1956
	b) The Virgin's head, detail of the triptych *The Virgin in the Church* by Jan van Eyck, Dresden, Staatliche Kunstsammlungen (M 5×)	B	L 7 074	1958

LXV.	a) The Child's head (M 5×)	B	L 5 787	1956
	b) The Child's head, detail of the triptych *The Virgin in the Church*, by Jan van Eyck, Dresden, Staatliche Kunstsammlungen (M 5×)	B	L 7 073	1958
LXVI.	The *Madonna and Child*, private Collection, Rome	B	184 429	1960
LXVII.	The *Holy Maidens*, detail from the *Adoration of the Lamb* by van Eyck, Ghent, Cathedral of S. Bavo, X-radiograph (1:1)	D	L 7 100	1971
LXVIII.	a) The *Madonna and Child in a Room*, Collegiate Church, Covarrubias		Photo Mas Barcelona	
	b) Unidentified wax seal on the back of the Melbourne panel (M 3× approx.)	A	111 045	1956

133

A. CLASSIFICATION IN THE CORPUS

No. 133: GROUP MARMION (4), *THE VIRGIN AND CHILD AT HALF-LENGTH*

B. IDENTIFYING REFERENCES

Marmion (Simon)
The Virgin and Child
No. 3079/4 in the *Catalogue of European Paintings before Eighteen Hundred, National Gallery of Victoria*, Melbourne, 1967 ([7] 81-82).

C. PHYSICAL CHARACTERISTICS
(14-XII-56)

Form: Rectangular.

Dimensions: Panel $\qquad$ 38,1 × 28 × 0,7 cm
$\qquad$ 15 × 11 × $\frac{5}{16}$ ins
$\qquad$ Painted surface 37,6 × 27,7 cm
$\qquad$ $14\frac{13}{16}$ × $10\frac{15}{16}$ ins

Protective Layer: A thin layer of modern varnish in good condition; ultra-violet rays show some patches or an older coat of varnish above the balustrade on either side of the Madonna.

Paint Layer: In fair condition despite a number of re-paints; the infra-red and X ray photographs (Pl. LXX and LXXI) reveal numerous restorations of which the most noticeable are in the sky, along the left border, in the hood and hair of the Madonna and around the contour of her face.

Changes in Composition: None noticed.

Ground: Thin, adhering well; paint losses reveal a buff coloured ground.

Support: Oak, single panel, simple modern cradling (Pl. XLVIII b).

Marks on the Back: Nothing worth recording.

Frame: Gothic, not original.

D. DESCRIPTION AND ICONOGRAPHY

1. *Subject*

The Virgin is seated on a chair with pine cone decoration on the arm rests, in front of a balustrade; the Child rests on her arms, her hands are folded in prayer; there is a cushion on her lap. Two columns above the balustrade divide into three the opening through which is a view of a landscape with rocks and a lake or wide river; churches with spires and cities appear in the middle, far and very far distance respectively (Pl. LXXII). The Child Christ seems to look at the spectator, perhaps to show him the breast of the Virgin (cf. *J. S. Held*, review of *Colin Tobias Eisler, Corpus New England*, in *The Art Bulletin*, Vol. XLIV, 1962, p. 345). The outward direction of the Child's glance and the centralized perspective of the chair arms may indicate that the panel was not part of a diptych. The picture is one of many derived with more or less change (and more or less directly) from the *Madonna of S. Luke* by Rogier van der Weyden (*Colin Tobias Eisler, New England Museums* (*Les Primitifs flamands*, I. *Corpus de la peinture des anciens Pays-Bas méridionaux au quinzième siècle*, 4), Brussels, 1961, No. 73(8), pl. LXXIX). Comparable points are

a) the Madonna with head bent to the right, wavy hair, a kerchief across the chest;

b) the three openings with two columns and a straight entablature above.

Certain features remind one of other works by Rogier:

a) The Child Christ is rather similar to that in the *Madonna with four Saints* (Staedel Institute, Frankfurt; *E. Panofsky, Early Netherlandish Painting. Its Origins and Character*, Cambridge, Mass., 1953, II, pl. 194, fig. 332);

b) praying hands in association with a half-figure "Madonna lactans" occur in the Caen *Madonna* (*M. J. Friedländer, Early Netherlandish Painting*, Vol. II, *Rogier van der Weyden and the Master of Flémalle*, Leyden/Brussels, 1967, No. 31, pl. 52); praying hands pointing downwards were used by Rogier in his triptych of the *Life of the Virgin*, Berlin, Ehem. Staatliche Museen, No. 534 A, *Holy Family* (*E. Panofsky, op. cit.*, pl. 181, fig. 319), or in the *Bladelin* altarpiece, Berlin, Ehem. Staatliche Museen, No. 535 (*E. Panofsky, op. cit.*, pl. 198, fig. 337). For the iconography of the "Madonna Lactans" see *Hélène Adhémar, Le Musée national du Louvre, Paris* (*Corpus de la peinture des anciens Pays-Bas méridionaux au quinzième siècle*, 5), I, Brussels, 1962, No. 83(11), p. 49.

2. *Colours*

The Virgin has red-brown hair and is in a blue mantle with thin gold border, a white kerchief and blue dress with grey fur border at the neckline and wrists. The cushion on her lap is green. Behind her, brown marble columns and grey masonry and capitals. The landscape is in light grey-browns, blue-greens and blue; the blue sky lightens to yellow-white towards the horizon.

3. *Inscriptions and Heraldry*

None.

E. ORIGIN AND SUBSEQUENT HISTORY
(FACTUAL EVIDENCE AND OPINIONS OF CRITICS)

1. *Origin*

a. *Factual Evidence*

The origin of the picture is not known; the first reference to it seems to be of 1885 (see E 2. a, *Subsequent History*).

b. *Opinions concerning Attribution and Date*

If identical with a picture exhibited at the *Orphelins d'Alsace-Lorraine* exhibition, Paris, 1885, No. 179, it was attributed then to Jan van Eyck; and it was certainly attributed to Jan van Eyck in Braun's catalogue of 1887 ([1] 114, No. 25; see also E 2. a). *Winkler* listed it in 1930 as a replica of the *Madonna and Child* by Simon Marmion which in 1927 was in the possession of Kleinberger and Goudstikker, Amsterdam ([2] 123). Accepted by *Ring* as by Marmion but still described as a replica of the Goudstikker picture ([3] 220, No. 176). *Bautier* ([5] 8, No. 12) believed the Melbourne Madonna to be derived from the *Madonna of S. Luke* by Rogier and attributed it to the Master of the S. Ursula Legend. *E. M. Hoffman*, in *Simon Marmion*, London, 1958 (Thesis presented at the Courtauld Institute, London, unpublished), referred to the Goudstikker picture as a replica of the Melbourne painting. *Hoffman* (*loc. cit.*) also suggested a date of 1465-75. Date and attribution were accepted by *U. Hoff* in 1961 ([6] 81-82) and in 1967 ([7] 81-82).

2. Subsequent History

a. Records concerning Ownership

1885   The panel is perhaps identical with No. 179 in the *Orphelins d'Alsace-Lorraine* exhibition at Paris, owned by Prince Czartoryski ("La Vierge et l'Enfant Jésus", no description, size 35 × 28 cm).

1887   In the Galerie Czartoryski, Paris, according to Braun's Catalogue ([1] 114, No. 25).

1930   In the Czartoryski Collection, Cracow, Poland as stated by *Winkler* ([2] 123).

1939   Taken to Paris by Count Czartoryski (information given by the Marlborough Gallery, London; on files of National Gallery of Victoria).

1950   Exhibition *La Vierge dans l'Art français*, Paris, lent from a "collection particulière" ([4] No. 39, pl. 46).

1954   On offer by the Marlborough Gallery, London and acquired by the Felton Bequest for the National Gallery of Victoria (*Hoff* [7] 82).

b. Records of Condition and Treatment

re 1887   Braun's photograph (a copy from the archives of M. J. Friedländer is now in the Rijksbureau voor Kunsthistorische Documentatie (R.K.D.) at The Hague) shows that the picture had been coarsely repainted at some time before 1887.

en 1887
d 1950   No records available, but it must have been cleaned and restored at some time between 1887 and 1950.

F. COMPARATIVE MATERIAL

(1) A close replica, 14½×10½ ins (36×26 cm), in which a red brocade hanging fills the space between the two columns behind the Madonna, was in a sale of various properties in Brussels, 12.XII.1924, lot. 9, repr. (as "Flemish school"); in 1926 the picture was at Douwes Bros., Amsterdam, No. 3700 (photograph Friedländer Archives, R.K.D., The Hague); it was exhibited at the Royal Academy of Arts, London, 1927 (Cat. No. 69, owner M. J. Goudstikker, Amsterdam) until March 5th, and in October 1927 in the *French Primitives* Exhibition, New York, No. 18, as "lent by F. Kleinberger Galleries". The picture was discussed by *Edouard Michel* (*A propos de Simon Marmion*, in *Gazette des Beaux-Arts*, Paris, 5th ser., Vol. XVI, 1927, p. 142) as the work of Simon Marmion. On the photograph (in the R.K.D., The Hague) made while the picture was at Douwes Bros, *Friedländer* has written: "mir im original vorgel. Kd stark verrieben, Haar d. Mad. neu. Brokat und Landschaft gut erhalten" [shown to me in the original; Child badly rubbed; hair of the Virgin new. Brocade and landscape well preserved].

(2) *A Madonna and Child* (Collection Kleiweg de Zwaan, Blaricum) is attributed by *Ring* to Simon Marmion ([3] No. 178). This has some similarity to the picture at Melbourne, but may be thought to be derived rather

from the *Madonna and Child* formerly in the Renders Collection (Tournai, Musée des Beaux-Arts; *M. J. Friedländer, Early Netherlandish Painting*, II. *Rogier van der Weyden and the Master of Flémalle*, Leyden/Brussels, 1967, pl. 50) or from some other, similar derivation from Rogier's *Virgin and Child with S. Luke* (*Meesterwerken uit vier eeuwen. 1400-1800. Tentoonstelling van Schilderijen en Teekeningen uit Particuliere Verzamelingen in Nederland, Museum Boymans – Rotterdam. 25 Juni-15 October 1938*, Rotterdam, 1938, pl. 18, fig. 20).

G. AUTHORS' COMMENTS

The picture seems to belong to the group of works connected with the *S. Bertin altarpiece* attributed to Simon Marmion (*Ring* [3] pl. 103) for the following reasons:

1. The closely related "Goudstikker" replica (see under F. 1.) has a brocade hanging behind the Madonna, the pattern of which closely resembles in reverse that of the hanging behind the donor Guillaume Fillastre on the left shutter of the *S. Bertin altarpiece* (*Ring* [3] pl. 104).

2. There are certain stylistic resemblances between the Melbourne picture and the *S. Bertin altarpiece*. The face of the Madonna may be compared with that of the angel above Guillaume Fillastre in the panel just mentioned; the long nose, the high curve of the eyebrows, the pointed oval chin, the hair held back by a black ribbon over a high forehead, are points of resemblance.

3. The landscape may be compared with that in the *S. Bertin altarpiece* in the panel of the *Dedication and building of a new monastery* (*Ring* [3] pl. 103, last on right); note the lake in the distance with rocky promontories jutting into it.

Comparison may also be made between the rock in the left middle distance and one occuring in a miniature attributed to Simon Marmion in fol. 388 of Ms. 9232 of the Bibliothèque Royale in Brussels, which was shown in the exhibition *Le Siècle d'Or de la Miniature flamande*, Brussels, 1959, Catalogue No. 59, pl. 3; here we also find rocks set in water and among the buildings a tower topped by a narrower round tower and crowned by a small spire; the miniature also shows luminous blues, greys and grey-greens, which with due restriction may be compared with those in the Melbourne painting.

H. BIBLIOGRAPHY

1887 [1]: A. D. BRAUN & CIE., *Catalogue général des Photographies*, Paris, 1887.

1930 [2]: FRIEDRICH WINKLER, *Marmion, Simon*, in *Allgemeines Lexikon der Bildenden Künstler von der Antike bis zur Gegenwart* (begründet von ULRICH THIEME und FELIX BECKER), Leipzig, XXIV, 1930, 122-123.

1949 [3]: GRETE RING, *A Century of French Painting. 1400-1500*, London, 1949.

1950 [4]: *La Vierge dans l'Art français*, Petit Palais, Paris, 1950.

1956 [5]: PIERRE BAUTIER, *Le Maître brugeois de la Légende de sainte Ursule*, in *Bulletin des Musées royaux des Beaux-Arts* (Brussels), Vol. V, 1956, 2-12.

1961 [6]: URSULA HOFF, *Catalogue of European Paintings before Eighteen Hundred. National Gallery of Victoria*, Melbourne, 1961.

1967 [7]: URSULA HOFF, *Catalogue of European Paintings before Eighteen Hundred. National Gallery of Victoria*, 2nd, enlarged ed., Melbourne, 1967.

J. LIST OF PLATES

A. CLASSIFICATION IN THE CORPUS

No. 134: GROUP MEMLINC (15), *THE MAN OF SORROWS IN THE ARMS OF THE VIRGIN*

B. IDENTIFYING REFERENCES

Memling (Hans)
The Man of Sorrows in the Arms of the Virgin
Dated 1475
No. 1335/3 in the *Catalogue of European Paintings before Eighteen Hundred. National Gallery of Victoria*, Melbourne, 1967 ([27] 83-85).

C. PHYSICAL CHARACTERISTICS
(14-XII-56)

Form: Rectangular.

Dimensions: Panel and painted surface $27,4 \times 19,9 \times 1$ cm
$10\frac{13}{16} \times 7\frac{7}{8} \times \frac{3}{8}$ ins

Protective Layer: A thin layer of modern varnish, in good condition.

Paint Layer: Very good general condition; remains of barbe on three sides, but no unpainted edge; inside the barbe there is a groove as if pressed in by a frame (Pl. LXXVI). That the panel has been cut down at some stage is suggested by the top edge where there is no barbe and the paint edge is chipped in places and unevenly cut away; for parts of the composition probably missing see G. *Authors' Comments*, p. 62.

Infra-red (Pl. LXXVII) and X-ray (Pl. LXXX-LXXXI) reveal no damage apart from small paint losses, the most noticeable of which occurs on the l. hand side on the capital, next to the 1 of the date. A large fill-in is to be found in the 2nd fold (from the top) of the linen sheet on the right hand side; yellow overpaint covers an area above the hat with the crown on the upper right and to the right of the nail closest to the edge. This paint has spilt over on the wooden slip which surrounds the panel.

Date on capital **1475** (1475) (Pl. LXXXII) is drawn in gold lines, and is in rather rubbed state (see further under G. *Authors' Comments*). Evidence of rubbing also on the red trickles of blood on Christ's forehead and side.

Changes in Composition: Infra-red photographs (Pl. LXXVII and LXXVIII) reveal considerable underdrawing, principally in the main figures, done with a metallic point. Numerous tentative strokes indicate light and dark as well as outlining forms. The artist works at first with free strokes, and finally precises more clearly the definitive outline. There are numerous pentimenti, the most noticeable of which are

a) Christ's left thumb was first to have had a position more to the right;

b) the hand that collects the blood was to have had a longer and more upright small finger;

c) it is possible that there have been alterations to the contour of the face on the left side;

d) the kerchief of the Madonna originally ended (by Christ's neck) in a horizontal line (for comment on the pentimenti, see under G. *Authors' Comments*).

Ground: Thin, adhering well; looks whitish at spots where there are paint losses.

Support: Oak, single panel, with vertical grain (Pl. XLVIII c).

Marks on the Back: Nothing worth reporting.

Frame: Not original.

D. DESCRIPTION AND ICONOGRAPHY

1. *Subject*

The main group is not a direct illustration of any event in the Passion of Christ, but elements of it correspond with details in illustrations of the Crucifixion and Lamentation. The side wound is referred to only in *S. John*, XIX, 34. The majority of the small illustrations on the background are derived from references in the story of Christ's Passion according to *S. Matthew* XXVI and XXVII and the other gospels.

Christ at half-length, crowned with thorns, with an aureole of faint rays, His eyes open, presses His left hand under the Wound on the right side of His body; the right arm hangs down, the hand is turned in and catches the blood that flows from the Wound. He is held in a linen sheet in the arms of the Virgin shown apparently with traces of a halo who stands behind Him. The figures are set against a gold ground on which appear symbols of the Passion: at the left the column, round which a tied cord holds a scourge with three thongs and a birch; above the capital appears the bust of Judas with his purse hanging from his neck. Higher up, the busts of what appear to be S. Peter and the Maid. Below them and to the right of Judas, two male busts. Below again, three right hands; an open hand, seen from the back, striking; a clenched hand clutching some hidden object, the string of which runs across the fingers; and lowest, a third hand with fingers pressed together. Further to the right, the reed with sponge and the lance, both leaning against the horizontal beam of the Cross, over which hangs, behind the Virgin on the right, the purple garment of Christ. At the extreme upper right, a turbaned head and a head wearing a hat with a crown. Below, a hand making the fica gesture; a hammer; the bust of a hatless, rough looking man in profile; below him a hand holding hair; a foot kicking and, lowest, three nails.

The Main Group

In varying association Christ as an image of pity, whether with eyes closed in death or (as here) with eyes open, has a long tradition; there are for instance in early Netherlandish painting many examples of Christ in this form in representations of the Trinity (see *H. Adhémar, Le Musée National du Louvre (Les Primitifs flamands,* I. *Corpus de la peinture des anciens Pays-Bas méridionaux au quinzième siècle*, 5), I, Brussels, 1962, p. 74). Perhaps under the influence of the Throne of Grace, the Virgin's head does not appear near Christ's but above it (see *von der Osten* [15] 470). *Schiller* ([29] 226, fig. 732) works out a parallel between the main group, the Throne of Grace, the "Engelpietà" and some Lamentations with the Virgin alone. This image is often associated with representations of a selection of the Instruments of the Passion, known as the *Arma Christi*, because they are sometimes represented heraldically. Important articles in this connection, in the first two of which the Melbourne painting is discussed, are by *Panofsky* ([7] 261-308), *Berliner* ([19] 35-152, fig. 8 etc. for heraldic representations) and *J. de Borchgrave d'Altena* (*La Messe de saint Grégoire*, in the *Bulletin des Musées Royaux des Beaux-Arts de Belgique* (Brussels), Vol. VIII, 1959, p. 3-34).

The treatment of the main group varies so much in different representations that it is undesirable to do more here than comment on a few special points:

a) Here, Christ is supported by the Virgin, which is quite frequent and is in particular recorded for a composition stated to be by Rogier van der Weyden (see G. *Authors' Comments*); it is indeed natural that the Virgin should be shown associated with the dead Christ in subjects partly comparable with the present subject such as Depositions and Entombments and it may be claimed that her prominent and centralised position here was meant to suggest to the spectator that the theme of the picture includes the sorrow of the Virgin as well as the suffering of Christ (*Berliner* [19] 76, note 437).

b) In Entombments or in the Taking down from the Cross and similar scenes Christ is often shown with curled up fingers (so in the variant of a Memlinc *Deposition* at Granada, exhibited at the *Memling Exhibition*, Bruges, 1939, No. 17 and pl. 34, but also often earlier); in the Melbourne picture the cupped hand receives the blood from the wound: as if taking the place of a chalice, which indeed appears often in representations of this or comparable subjects (e.g. *Panofsky* [7] fig. 41 or a woodcut of about 1470 where Christ holds the chalice under his wound, considered to be from Ulm, *Schreiber* No. 877).

Other examples of Christ receiving the blood in His hand are in a picture ascribed to Colyn de Coter in The Mount Trust Collection, Churchill, Oxfordshire (reproduced in *Le Siècle de Bruegel. La Peinture en Belgique au XVI*ᵉ *siècle. Musées royaux des Beaux-Arts de Belgique*, Brussels, 1963, No. 82, fig. 11); at Pedralbes (reproduced *Catálogo Monumental de España. La Ciudad de Barcelona*, by *J. Ainaud, J. Gudiol* and *F. P. Verrié*, Barcelona, 1947, fig. 842); in the Capilla del Condestable, Burgos Cathedral (*J. Lavalleye, Collections d'Espagne* (*Les Primitifs flamands*, II. *Répertoire des Peintures flamandes des quinzième et seizième siècles*, 2), Antwerp, 1958, p. 30, No. 78 and pl. XVIII); in the Georges Platteau Collection, Tournai, *Christ in the Arms of an Angel*, presumed to be of the late 15th century, Anonymous (*Tournai, Halle aux draps. Exposition des Arts religieux anciens et modernes du 13 août au 16 septembre 1949*, s.l., 1949, p. 88, No. 9; *Scaldis* Exhibition, Tournai, Halle aux draps, Casino communal, etc., from July 15 to September 10, 1956, No. 17*bis* of the Section *Peinture;* A.C.L. Photo No. 165.694 B); *Christ between the Virgin and S. John with Saints and Angels*, Bruges, Musée des Hospices, No. 14 (A.C.L. Photo No. 112.380 B).

The Background Illustrations

The meaning of most of the small illustrations on the gold ground is evident; comment will be made on certain points.

a) *Weale* recorded at the top of the column "the board with the title I.N.R.I." but he seems to have done so in error ([1] 75).

When (as frequently) the column is shown, it is often surmounted by the cock (as in the variant of the present picture in Granada, *Van Schoute* [26] No. 97 and pl. CXIV) and is rarely surmounted by any other emblem of the Passion (though the hand holding hair is in this position in some woodcuts of the *Mass of S. Gregory*: *Schreiber*, Nos. 1467 etc.; a woodcut reproduced by *Borchgrave d'Altena, op. cit.*, fig. 10). Here the cock is missing altogether and the column is surmounted by the head of Judas; it is to be noted that this association occurs in versions of a *Mass of S. Gregory* often connected with the Master of Flémalle (one *M. J. Friedländer, Early Nether-landish Painting*, Vol. II. *Rogier van der Weyden and the Master of Flémalle*, Leyden/Brussels, 1967, No. 73 a and his Plate 100; the other, *Friedländer* No. 73 b, reproduced by *J. Moreira Freire, Un Problème d'Art, L'Ecole Portu-gaise Créatrice des Grandes Ecoles*, Lisbon, 1898, p. 174, and apparently identical with a picture now in the Museum at Brussels, reproduced in *The Art Quarterly*, Vol. IX, 1946, p. 174 and by *Friedländer, op. cit.*, Add. 150, pl. 100). The great rarity of this association is perhaps underlined by the fact that the usual cock takes the place of Judas in a variant of this *Mass of S. Gregory* by the Westphalian Master of 1473, in the church of S. Maria zur Wiese at Soest (reproduced in the catalogue *Westfälische Maler der Spätgotik, 1440-1490. Landesmuseum für Kunst und Kulturgeschichte. Münster, Westfalen. 20. Juni-30. September 1952*, (Münster, 1952), No. 234, pl. 64).

b) *Weale* ([1] 75) interpreted the two busts on the left hand side as Annas and Caiaphas and the two on the right hand side as Pilate and Herod, which seems plausible. These names are inscribed against heads in similar positions on the background of the *Mass of S. Gregory*, in a "Nederlandse Getijdenboek" (*A. W. Byvanck* and *G. J. Hooge-werff, Noord-Nederlandsche Miniaturen in handschriften der 14e, 15e en 16e eeuwen*, The Hague, 1922, pl. 14). *Richard Morris* (*Legends of the Holy Rood*, London, 1871, p. 188) gives illustrations of profile faces by the side of the face of Christ, which may be compared with the profile head on the right, the text being: "*Judeus spuens in facie Christi*", "*The Jew that spat in God's face*". The motif is frequent; it may be related to *Isaiah* (L, 6): "*I hid not my face from shame and spitting*". Other profile heads spitting occur for example

1. in the above mentioned *Mass of S. Gregory* in the "Nederlandse Getijdenboek" (*Byvanck* and *Hoogewerff*, *op. cit.*, pl. 14); here the man in profile next to Christ is shown spitting and is accompanied by the inscription "*Spuiver*";

2. among the emblems of the Passion on the bosses on the vault of the quire of Winchester Cathedral, ascribed to the period 1503-9 (*C. J. P. Cave, The Bosses on the Vault of the Quire of Winchester Cathedral*, in *Archaeologia*, Vol. LXXVI, 1926-27, p. 167, No. 26, pl. XXVIII, fig. 9).

c) The open right hand seen from the back appears with the inscription "*manus dans alapas*" in a manuscript at Brussels (Bibliothèque royale, Ms. 4459.70, fol. 192v), stated to be of 1320 (*Berliner* [19] 49, fig. 4). Similarly in *Richard Morris, op. cit.*, where are included illustrations of symbols of the Passion with ancient descriptions, on p. 177 there is shown an open hand from the back together with a hand clutching hair, with the accom-panying text (modernized): "*The hand Lord that tore off Thine hair and the hand that clapped Thee under the ear*". Further to the hand shown clutching hair in this picture, this is seen among the Passion emblems on the bosses of the vault of the quire of Winchester Cathedral, and described by the author as a reference to *Isaiah* (L, 6): "*I gave my back to the smiters and my cheek to them that plucked off the hair*" (*Cave, op. cit.*, p. 168, boss 46, pl. XXIX, fig. 7). Although the clutching or tearing out of Christ's hair is not recorded in the gospels, this is frequently shown in illustrations of various scenes of the Passion, e.g. *Christ taken Prisoner* (engravings by the Master der Weibermacht, L. I. 73, 2 and Schongauer, B 10), *Christ before Annas* (Schongauer engraving, B 11), *The Flagellation* (Memlinc's picture at Turin and Schongauer's engraving, B 12) and, to cite an earlier, Italian example, *The Mocking of Christ* (Giotto's fresco at Padua); see *M. Geisberg, Die Anfänge des Kupferstichs* (*Meister der Graphik, II*), Leipzig, 1923, pl. 16; *M. Lehrs, Martin Schongauer* (*Graphische Gesellschaft, V*), Berlin, 1914, pls. IX, X, XI (about 1470-80); *C. Aru, Et. de Geradon, La Galerie Sabauda de Turin* (*Les Primitifs flamands, I. Corpus de la peinture des anciens Pays-Bas méridionaux au quinzième siècle*, 2), Antwerp, 1952, p. 14, No. 18, pl. XXIX; *R. Van Marle, The Development of the Italian Schools of Painting*, Vol. III, The Hague, 1924, fig. 56.

Weale ([1] 75) interpreted the clenched hand, on the left under the striking hand, as that of Judas grasping the purse. This is made likely by the presence of the string.

d) The kicking foot appears to be rare; but what seems acceptable as another example (though the foot there is not shown as actually kicking) is in the already mentioned Fig. 4 of *Berliner*'s article inscribed *"trusio pedum"* (*Berliner* [19] 49); a kicking leg occurs in the *Lamentation with the Instruments of the Passion*, Messina, Museo Nazionale (*Carandente* [28] 40-41, No. 25, pl. XX). The motif occurs occasionally in the Carrying of the Cross, for example in the painting by the Master of the Virgo inter Virgines, Barnard Castle (*G. J. Hoogewerff, De Noord-Nederlandsche Schilderkunst*, Vol. 2, The Hague, 1937, p. 259, fig. 123) or in Barent van Orley, *The Carrying of the Cross*, reproduced in *M. J. Friedländer, Die altniederländische Malerei*, Vol. XIV, *Pieter Bruegel und Nachträge zu den früheren Bänden*, Leyden, 1937, pl. Nachtr. XXVII.

2. *Colours*

The Virgin is in white kerchief and dark blue mantle; her eyes are light grey-brown. Christ is held in a white linen sheet striped with blue; His tunic hanging on the cross appears a very dark purple; His eyes are light brown, His hair dark brown. The crown of thorns is a greyish black; the *Arma Christi* appear on a gold ground dotted with red and black towards the edges and along the contour of the column. The column of martyrdom is brown with a grey-green capital. Yellow, green, red and black are used in the garments of the busts among the *arma* (See further G. *Authors' Comments* and Pl. LXXVII A).

3. *Inscriptions and Heraldry*

Inscribed on the capital of the column in gold **1 4 7 5** (1475) (Pl. LXXXII). This date has been read 1473 by *Cazier* and *Delevoy* ([17] 423) and 1474 by a few authors (*R. P. B.* [6] 52; *Panofsky* [7] 275; *Catalogue of the National Gallery of Victoria* [14] 102, No. 428).

E. ORIGIN AND SUBSEQUENT HISTORY
(FACTUAL EVIDENCE AND OPINIONS OF CRITICS)

1. *Origin*

a. *Factual Evidence*

The origin of this picture is unknown but it bears the date of 1475 (see above).
The picture did not become known until 1905; see under E. 2, *Subsequent History*.

b. *Opinions concerning Attribution and Date*

Weale, who published the picture for the first time in 1905 ([1] 75), attributed it to a Master of Tournai. The picture was given to Memlinc by *von Loga* ([2] 52), who judged it is of better quality than another version of the same subject in the Capilla Real in Granada (see F. *Comparative Material* and G. *Authors' Comments*); this last version was attributed to Memlinc by *Carl Justi* in 1890 (*Aus der Capilla Real zu Granada*, in *Zeitschrift für christliche Kunst* (Düsseldorf), Vol. III, 1890, p. 205).
Friedländer ([3] 165; [4] 57; [5] 57; [20] 42-43) considered the possibility that entries in the inventories of the art treasures belonging to Margaret of Austria drawn up in 1516 and 1524 (see I. *Transcriptions of Documents and Literary*

Sources, Documents 1 and *2*, p. 65) may refer to this picture; but he doubted this then, on the ground that the picture in Margaret of Austria's inventory of 1516 is unlikely to have been wrongly attributed to Rogier van der Weyden, and stressed this doubt more later ([8] 17-18; [13] 5-6; [31] 14-15). This picture is more probably a free copy of a lost panel by Rogier. The attribution to Memlinc is not known ever to have been questioned except by *Panofsky* ([7] 274-275, 298, note 32); though he judged the Melbourne version is better than that of Granada. See *R. P. B.* ([6] 52), *M. J.* ([9] 33), *Cordonnier-Détrie* ([10] 105-106), *Tombu* ([11] 177), *Cazier* and *Delevoy* ([17] 423), *Gallego y Burín* ([18] 82), *Berliner* ([19] 76, 136, note 437), *Lavalleye* ([21] 23), *Eisler* ([22] 42), *Hoff* ([23] 83-85), *Tomory* ([25] 50) and *Van Schoute* ([26] 62-63).

Hulin de Loo, who saw the picture prior to cleaning at Agnew's (before 1924, see E. 2), called it "a characteristic work of Memling and of high quality" (*Frank Rinder*, correspondence 21 May, 1924, National Gallery of Victoria files).

Except for the problem of the reading (see above, D. 3, *Inscriptions and Heraldry*), the date is not known so far to have been questioned (see G. *Authors' Comments*).

2. *Subsequent History*

a. *Records concerning Ownership*

1900/5   Purchased by Théodore Griveau of Connerré, Sarthe, France, from a 'brocanteur' in Caen (*Cordonnier-Détrie* [10] 105-106); published by *Weale* ([1] 75), who had seen the painting in the collection of Griveau.

or later   Possibly on the Berlin art market, deduced from a doubtful statement (*Cordonnier-Détrie* [10] 105).

a. 1921   Apparently at Thomas Agnew's, London (*Friedländer* [5] 188, printed "Aquer & Sons").

1924   It is recorded in *Gimpel's* diary ([24] 263), that the picture had been bought by Count Sala, representative of Agnew's in Paris, from 'a kind of peasant' who lived in central France, had a series of Primitives and well understood the value of this picture.

Acquired from Agnew's by the Felton Bequest for the National Gallery of Victoria, Melbourne. Exhibited at the National Gallery, London, from April to June of that year before its departure to Melbourne (*R. P. B.* [6] 52).

b. *Records of Condition and Treatment*

e 1924   When the panel was at Agnew's, it was cleaned (*Frank Rinder*, correspondence 21 May, 1924, National Gallery of Victoria files).

1924   In 1924 it has been judged carefully cleaned and apparently in very good condition, by *R. P. B.* ([6] 52). Has not been cleaned since it came to Melbourne. As has been noted the picture seems to have been cut at the top; see further under G. *Authors' Comments*.

F. COMPARATIVE MATERIAL

(1) A closely related composition, but by no means a copy of our painting, is in the Capilla Real in Granada (53,4×38 cm), discussed by *Van Schoute* ([26] 58-64, pl. CXIV-CXX) and attributed to Memlinc and his studio.

(2) Another version, related to 1. with variations, is the *Vierge de Pitié* (73×58 cm) attributed to a Burgundian studio, which belongs to the Church of Cormatin, Saône-et-Loire, France. It seems first to have been discussed by *Pierre Dalloz* (*Une trouvaille*, in the *Revue du Touring Club de France*, Paris, December 1929, p. 289), according to whom it had belonged to Cardinal Thomas, Archbishop of Rouen (who died ca. 1894/5); it was exhibited

in *La Vierge dans l'Art Français*, Paris, 1950, No. 44 and pl. 50; and the catalogue adds the information that it was given to the church at Cormatin by Paul Thomas, nephew of the Archbishop. This version is discussed by *Van Schoute* [26] 61, (F. 3).

(3) A version related to 1. is at Bilbao, Museo de Bellas Artes, from the de Jado collection (panel, 31×21 cm); a photograph in the Friedländer Archives, R.K.D., The Hague and photograph from the Museo, D 791 B; see *Friedländer* [8] 123, No. 37 b; [31] 51, No. 37 b, pl. 89; *Van Schoute* [26] 61, (F. 2).

(4) Kleinberger version, *Friedländer* [8] 123, No. 37 c; [31] 51, No. 37 c, pl. 89; *Van Schoute* [26] 61, (F. 4); photograph in the Friedländer Archives, R.K.D.; related to 1 and 3 in composition.

(5) Another version Rome, Principe Massimo, in 1932 with Bottenwieser, Berlin; a replica of the Melbourne composition, photograph in the Friedländer Archives, R.K.D., inscribed by him: *"ganz überarbeitet"*; *Van Schoute* [26] 62, (F. 5).

(6) A version of half the Melbourne composition is recorded in a photograph in the Friedländer Archives, inscribed *"VII, 55"*; the hands and wounds are not shown. Apparently of poor quality.

(7) A *Pietà* was listed in an anonymous sale at Christie's, London, March 29, 1935, No. 102, on panel, 8×6 ins. It is described as the Virgin supporting the Dead Saviour, with the Cross and figures of the Crucifixion on a gold background, so it was possibly a repetition of the Melbourne composition and perhaps identical with 5.

G. AUTHORS' COMMENTS

The absence of a barbe at the upper margin and the fact that in a replica of this picture (see F. 5) a small strip revealing the upper edge of the Cross and the dice lying on it may be seen, suggests that the picture has been trimmed a little at the top. The presumed reduction explains the absence of the top of the head of S. Peter and of the tip of the lance. It is also possible that the three dice, which frequently belong to the *arma*, were shown as in F. 5.

As for the date inscribed on the capital, it has not been proved on technical grounds that it is false, but it is suspect. Its execution in thin gold lines is at least curious; and it may be noted that the gold is slightly paler in colour than the gold of the background and that used for the rays behind Christ's head and what appears to be the remains of the Virgin's halo. Further, the position of the date in the picture raises doubt; Memlinc's inscribed paintings (such as *Friedländer* [31] Nos. 2, 11, 14) usually carry the year of execution on the frame. In the one known instance where a genuine date occurs in the painting itself (*Friedländer* [31] No. 23 B), the figures are represented as 'carved' into the stone sill; the figure 7 in this inscription differs from that in the Melbourne painting. In the *Madonna with Child and S. Anthony* (*Friedländer* [31] No. 64) the date 1472 situated in the painting itself is regarded by *Friedländer* and others as copied from the lost frame (*R. H. Hubbard, The National Gallery of Canada, Catalogue of Paintings and Sculpture*, Vol. I, Ottawa/Toronto, 1957, p. 64). For comment on these inscriptions, see *Flanders in the Fifteenth Century*, Exhibition at Detroit 1960, catalogue Nos. 30/31, and *Jacqueline Folie, Les Œuvres authentifiées des Primitifs flamands*, in the *Bulletin de l'Institut Royal du Patrimoine Artistique*, Vol. VI, 1963, p. 225-6.

It may be that the date of 1475 is correct for this picture; but in the authors' opinion, if this is the case, the original date is likely to have been put by Memlinc on the original frame and the existing date copied from this at some later time.

As *Van Schoute* has pointed out, the character of the preliminary drawing is strongly suggestive of Memlinc's creative work. The underdrawing is of a kind found in paintings by Memlinc. Compare for example infrared photographs of the *Marriage of S. Catherine* at Bruges, S. John's Hospital (in the archives of the Centre de Recherches "Primitifs flamands"); S. Barbara seated shows in the folds of her garment hatching that piles up to form the shading as under the left arm of Christ's here; unsystematic lines occur on face and neck of S. Barbara, similar to the lines appearing on the right arm of Christ. Pentimenti are, further, frequent in Memlinc's preparatory work.

Is the composition related to a picture by Rogier van der Weyden? In the inventories of Margaret of Austria is recorded a picture of the *Man of Sorrows* in the arms of the Virgin, by Rogier van der Weyden, the wings (whether original or added later) being by Master Hans, presumably Memlinc (see I. *Document 1*, p. 65). *Friedländer* ([8] 17-18; [31] 14-15) suggested that this composition by Rogier may have been the source of Memlinc's pictures of the subject in Granada and Melbourne. In this context one should consider an engraving by 'Monogrammist f', possibly of about 1470, of the same theme (*F. W. H. Hollstein, Dutch and Flemish Etchings, Engravings and Woodcuts*, Vol. XII, *Masters and Monogrammists of the 15th Century*, Amsterdam, n.d., p. 139; L. 1). The differences between the Melbourne and Granada paintings are considerable; yet they might all be derivatives, with varying degrees of freedom, from a common source, perhaps Rogier's painting. It is worth pointing out that there is a fairly close correspondence between the Melbourne painting and the engraving, in the body of Christ and in particular in the disposition of the arms and the left hand, but not the right hand. In the variant picture at Granada, the arms are disposed differently.

The symmetrical balance of the composition suggests that it was not part of a diptych. None of the existing repetitions and variants appear in diptych form. *Sánchez Cantón's* suggestion that the Granada variant was part of a diptych has not been supported by *Van Schoute* ([26] E. 2, a. b., p. 60). The picture in the possession of Margaret of Austria is described as a triptych.

H. BIBLIOGRAPHY

1905 [1]: W. H. James Weale, *The Image of Pity by an Unknown Master of the Fifteenth Century*, in *The Burlington Magazine* (London), Vol. VII, 1905, 75.

1910 [2]: Valerian von Loga, *Zum Altar von Miraflores*, in *Jahrbuch der königlich preuszischen Kunstsammlungen* (Berlin), Vol. XXXI, 1910, 47-56.

1913 [3]: (Max J. Friedländer), *Sitzungsbericht der Kunstgeschichtlichen Gesellschaft*, Berlin, Vol. V, 9 May, 1913, 164-167.

1916 [4]: Max J. Friedländer, *Von Eyck bis Bruegel. Studien zur Geschichte der Niederländischen Malerei*, Berlin, 1916.

1921 [5]: Max J. Friedländer, *Von Eyck bis Bruegel. Studien zur Geschichte der Niederländischen Malerei*, second ed., Berlin, 1921.

1924 [6]: R. P. B., *Sammlungen. Melbourne*, in *Monatsrundschau der Zeitschrift für bildende Kunst* (Leipzig), Vol. LVIII, October 1924, 52-53.

1927 [7]: Erwin Panofsky, *"Imago Pietatis". Ein Beitrag zur Typengeschichte des "Schmerzensmanns" und der "Maria Mediatrix"*, in *Festschrift für Max J. Friedländer zum 60. Geburtstage*, Leipzig, 1927, 261-308.

1928 [8]: MAX J. FRIEDLÄNDER, *Die Altniederländische Malerei*, VI. *Memling und Gerard David*, Berlin, 1928.

1929 [9]: M. J., *Revue des revues. La Pietà de Cormatin*, in *Beaux-Arts* (Paris), Vol. VII, 20-XII-1929, 33.

1930 [10]: PAUL CORDONNIER-DÉTRIE, *La Pietà de Cormatin et celle de Connerré*, in *Revue historique et archéologique du Maine* (Le Mans), 2nd ser., Vol. X, 1930, 105-109.

1930 [11]: JEANNE TOMBU [and] PL. LEFÈVRE, *Un diptyque de l'église Saint-Nicolas, à Bruxelles*, in *Annales de la Société Royale d'Archéologie de Bruxelles* (Brussels), Vol. XXXV, 1930, 175-178.

1932 [12]: E. LA TOUCHE ARMSTRONG and R. D. BOYS, *The Book of the Public Library, Museums and National Gallery of Victoria, 1906-1931*, Melbourne, 1932.

1943 [13]: MAX J. FRIEDLÄNDER, *Memling* (*Palet Serie*), Amsterdam, (1943).

1943 [14]: X., *Catalogue of the National Gallery of Victoria*, Melbourne, 1943.

1948 [15]: GERT VON DER OSTEN, *Beweinung Christi*, in *Reallexikon zur Deutschen Kunstgeschichte*, Stuttgart-Waldsee, II, 1948, 457-475.

1948 [16]: X., *Catalogue of the National Gallery of Victoria*, Melbourne, 1948.

1950 [17]: R. CAZIER and ROBERT L. DELEVOY, *Memlinc (Memling), Hans ou Jean*, in *Dictionnaire des Peintres*, Brussels, [1950], 419-425.

1952 [18]: ANTONIO GALLEGO Y BURÍN, *La Capilla Real de Granada*, 2nd ed., (Madrid, 1952).

1955 [19]: RUDOLF BERLINER, *Arma Christi*, in *Münchner Jahrbuch der bildenden Kunst* (Munich), 3rd ser., Vol. VI, 1955, 35-152.

1956 [20]: MAX J. FRIEDLÄNDER, *Early Netherlandish Painting from Van Eyck to Bruegel* (translated from the second German ed.), London, 1956.

1959 [21]: JACQUES LAVALLEYE, *Considérations sur les Primitifs flamands conservés à la Capilla Real de Grenade*, in *Académie royale de Belgique. Bulletin de la classe des Beaux-Arts* (Brussels), Vol. XLI, 1959, 21-29.

1961 [22]: COLIN TOBIAS EISLER, *New England Museums* (*Les Primitifs flamands*, I. Corpus de la peinture des anciens Pays-Bas méridionaux au quinzième siècle, 4), Brussels, 1961.

1961 [23]: URSULA HOFF, *Catalogue of European Paintings before Eighteen Hundred. National Gallery of Victoria*, Melbourne, 1961.

1963 [24]: R. GIMPEL, *Journal d'un collectionneur marchand de tableaux*, s.l., 1963.

1963 [25]: P. A. TOMORY, *Buchbesprechungen. Ursula Hoff, Catalogue of Paintings before 1800, National Gallery of Victoria, Melbourne*, [...], in *Pantheon* (Munich), Vol. XXI, 1963, 48-50.

1963 [26]: ROGER VAN SCHOUTE, *La Chapelle Royale de Grenade* (*Les Primitifs flamands*, I. Corpus de la peinture des anciens Pays-Bas méridionaux au quinzième siècle, 6), Brussels, 1963.

1967 [27]: URSULA HOFF, *Catalogue of European Paintings before Eighteen Hundred. National Gallery of Victoria*, 2nd, enlarged ed., Melbourne, 1967.

1968 [28]: GIOVANNI CARANDENTE, *Collections d'Italie*, I. *Sicile* (*Les Primitifs flamands*, II. Répertoire des peintures flamandes du quinzième siècle, 3), Brussels, 1968.

1968 [29]: GERTRUD SCHILLER, *Ikonographie der christlichen Kunst*, Vol. II. *Die Passion Jesu Christi*, Gütersloh, 1968.

1969 [30]: MARIA CORTI and GIORGIO T. FAGGIN, *L'opera completa di Memling* (*Classici dell'arte*, 27), Milan, 1969.

1971 [31]: MAX J. FRIEDLÄNDER, *Early Netherlandish Painting*, VI, Part. I. *Hans Memlinc and Gerard David*, Leyden/Brussels, 1971.

I. TRANSCRIPTIONS OF DOCUMENTS AND LITERARY SOURCES

1.

The Man of Sorrows in the arms of the Virgin, as a central panel of a triptych, mentioned in the inventory of the art treasures belonging to Margaret of Austria (1516).

Ung petit tableaul d'ung dieu de pityé estant ès bras de Nostre-Dame; ayant deux feulletz, dans chascun desquelz y a ung ange et dessus lesdits feulletz y a une annunciade de blanc et de noir. Fait, le tableaul, de la main de Rogier, et lesditz feulletz, de celle de maistre Hans.

(*Lille, Archives du Département du Nord, Ms. B 3507 (123 904), no foliated page. Published by* M. le Glay, Correspondance de l'empereur Maximilien Ier et de Marguerite d'Autriche, sa fille, gouvernante des Pays-Bas, de 1507 à 1519, publiée d'après les manuscrits originaux, *Vol. II, Paris, 1839, p. 480*).

2.

Idem, inventory of 1524.

124. Ung aultre tableau de Nostre Dame tenant Nostre Seigneur nuz devant elle, clouant à deux feuilletz, où il y a deux anges tenant l'ung une épée en sa main.

(*Paris, Bibliothèque nationale, Collection dite des 500 de Colbert. Published by* de Laborde, Inventaire des tableaux, livres, joyaux et meubles de Marguerite d'Autriche [...] fait et conclud en la ville d'Anvers le XVII d'avril M Vc XXIIII, *Paris, 1850, p. 23-24*).

J. LIST OF PLATES

No. 134: GROUP MEMLINC (15)

XLVIII.	c) The Man of Sorrows in the Arms of the Virgin, the Reverse	N.G.	10 014 E	1965
LXXVI.	The Man of Sorrows in the Arms of the Virgin	N.G.	10 009 E	1965
LXXVIIA.	*The Man of Sorrows in the Arms of the Virgin (Colour Plate)*	N.G.		1965
LXXVII.	The Man of Sorrows in the Arms of the Virgin, infra-red	ACL	L 5 922 E	1965
LXXVIII.	Detail of Christ's hands, infra-red (M $1\frac{1}{2}$ × approx.)	ACL	L 5 923 E	1965
LXXIX.	Detail of Christ's hands (M $1\frac{1}{2}$ × approx.)	N.G.	10 013 E	1965
LXXX.	The upper half, X-radiograph (1:1)	N.G.	10 067 E	1965
LXXXI.	The lower half, X-radiograph (1:1)	N.G.	10 067 E	1965
LXXXII.	The upper left corner (M 2×)	N.G.	10 010 E	1965
LXXXIII.	The background at right (M 2×)	N.G.	10 011 E	1965
LXXXIV.	Christ and Virgin, detail (M 2×)	N.G.	10 012 E	1965

INDICES

I. INDEX OF PERSONS AND PLACES

Names of places are in small capitals

II. INDEX OF SUBJECTS

RELIGIOUS SUBJECTS

PLATES

Pl. I

No. 131: Anonymous *(13), The Triptych with the Miracles of Christ*

Pl. II

No. 131: Anonymous *(13), The Triptych with the Miracles of Christ. Central panel, the figures and plants mentioned in the text*

Pl. III

No. 131: Anonymous *(13), The Triptych with the Miracles of Christ. Central panel, The Multiplication of the Loaves and Fishes*

Pl. IV

No. 131: Anonymous *(13), The Triptych with the Miracles of Christ. Central panel, the lower left corner*

Pl. V

No. 131: Anonymous *(13), The Triptych with the Miracles of Christ. Central panel, the lower right corner*

Pl. VI

No. 131: Anonymous (13), The Triptych with the Miracles of Christ. Central panel, the group of Christ and the Apostles in the middle distance on the right

Pl. VII

No. 131: Anonymous (13), The Triptych with the Miracles of Christ. Central panel, the multitude in the middle distance on the left and the miracles in the background

Pl. VIII

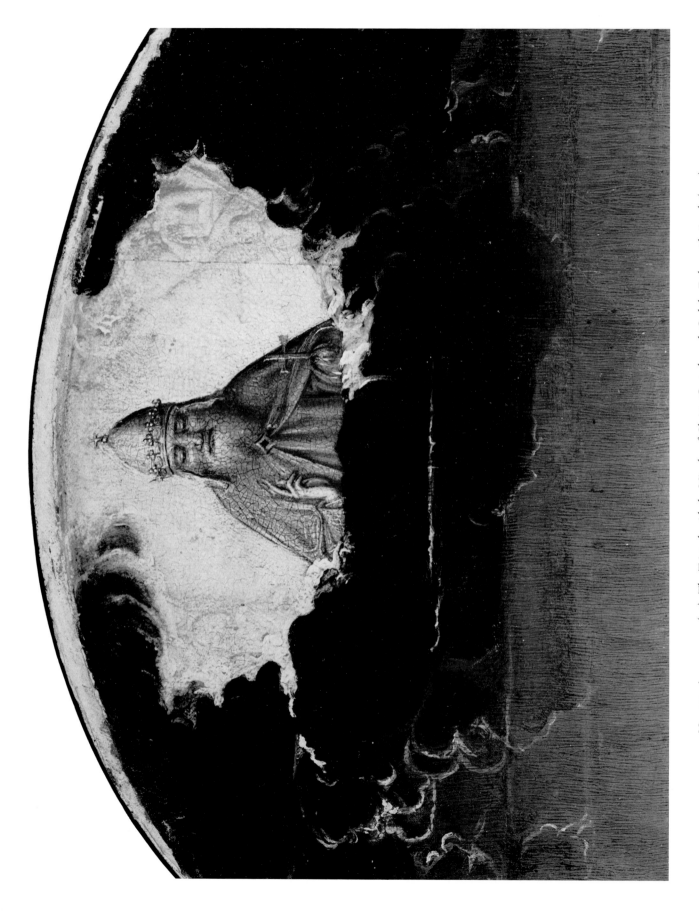

No. 131: Anonymous (13), The Triptych with the Miracles of Christ. Central panel, God the Father with Angels (1:1)

Pl. IX

Pl. X

No. 131: Anonymous (13), The Triptych with the Miracles of Christ
Central panel, busts of Jacoba of Bavaria (?) and John IV, Duke of Brabant (M 2×)

Pl. XI

No. 131: Anonymous *(13), The Triptych with the Miracles of Christ*
Central panel, busts of Philip of Saint Pol, Duke of Brabant and of a woman (M 2×)

Pl. XII

No. 131: Anonymous *(13), The Triptych with the Miracles of Christ*
Left wing, obverse, The Marriage at Cana, a) The whole; b) The figures identified in the text

Pl. XIII

No. 131: Anonymous (13), *The Triptych with the Miracles of Christ*
Left wing, obverse, The Marriage at Cana. The upper half

Pl. XIV

No. *131:* Anonymous *(13), The Triptych with the Miracles of Christ*
Left wing, obverse, The Marriage at Cana. The lower half

Pl. XV

No. 131: Anonymous (13), The Triptych with the Miracles of Christ
Left wing, obverse, The Marriage at Cana. Detail showing Philip the Fair and the table (1: 1)

Pl. XVI

No. 131: Anonymous (13), The Triptych with the Miracles of Christ. Left wing, obverse, The Marriage at Cana. The three wives of Philip the Good (1 : 1 approx.)

Pl. XVII

No. 131: Anonymous (13), The Triptych with the Miracles of Christ. Left wing, obverse, The Marriage at Cana. Engelbert II of Nassau (?) and Adolph of Cleves (1:1)

Pl. XVIII

No. *131*: Anonymous *(13), The Triptych with the Miracles of Christ*
Left wing, obverse, The Marriage at Cana. Philip the Good, Charles the Bold and Margaret of York (?) (1 : 1)

Pl. XIX

No. 131: Anonymous *(13), The Triptych with the Miracles of Christ. Left wing, obverse, The Marriage at Cana.*
Detail of architecture showing two niches with the serpent and Adam and Eve after the Fall

Pl. XX

No. 131: Anonymous (13), The Triptych with the Miracles of Christ
Right wing, obverse, The Raising of Lazarus, a) The whole; b) The figures and plants identified in the text

Pl. XXI

No. 131: Anonymous *(13), The Triptych with the Miracles of Christ*
Right wing, obverse, The Raising of Lazarus. The lower half

Pl. XXII

No. 131: Anonymous (13), The Triptych with the Miracles of Christ. Right wing, obverse, The Raising of Lazarus. Busts of Christ, a woman and some disciples

Pl. XXIII

No. 131: Anonymous *(13), The Triptych with the Miracles of Christ*
Right wing, obverse, The Raising of Lazarus. The house and the landscape in the background

Pl. XXIV

No. 131: Anonymous *(13), The Triptych with the Miracles of Christ*
The Reverse of the Triptych: a) The Repose on the Flight to Egypt; b) S. Peter

Pl. XXV

No. 131: Anonymous (13), The Triptych with the Miracles of Christ
Left wing, reverse, The Repose on the Flight to Egypt. The Virgin, Child and landscape

Pl. XXVI

No. 131: Anonymous *(13), The Triptych with the Miracles of Christ*
Left wing, reverse, The Repose on the Flight to Egypt. The Child

Pl. XXVII

No. 131: Anonymous *(13), The Triptych with the Miracles of Christ*
Left wing, reverse, The Repose on the Flight to Egypt. Detail of the landscape, infra-red

Pl. XXVIII

No. 131: Anonymous (13), The Triptych with the Miracles of Christ. Right wing, reverse, S. Peter. The upper part

Pl. XXIX

No. 131: Anonymous (13), The Triptych with the Miracles of Christ. Right wing, reverse, S. Peter. The middle part

Pl. XXX

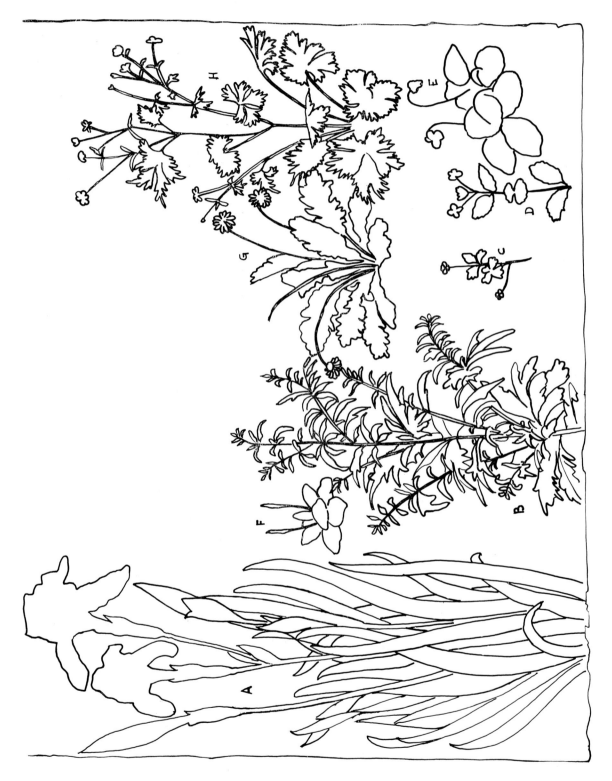

No. 131: Anonymous (13). The Triptych with the Miracles of Christ. Right wing, reverse, S. Peter. The plants identified on the lower part

Pl. XXXI

No. 131: Anonymous (13), The Triptych with the Miracles of Christ. Right wing, reverse, S. Peter. The lower part

Pl. XXXII

No. 131: Anonymous *(13), The Triptych with the Miracles of Christ
Right wing, reverse, S.Peter. Bust of the Saint*

Pl. XXXIII

No. 131: Anonymous *(13), The Triptych with the Miracles of Christ*
Right wing, reverse, S. Peter. Detail of the plants

Pl. XXXIV

No. 131: Anonymous *(13), The Triptych with the Miracles of Christ. Detail of the central panel, infra-red*

Pl. XXXV

No. 131: Anonymous *(13), The Triptych with the Miracles of Christ. Detail of the right wing obverse, infra-red*

Pl. XXXVI

No. 131: Anonymous *(13), The Triptych with the Miracles of Christ. Detail of the left wing obverse, infra-red*

Pl. XXXVII

No. 131: Anonymous *(13), The Triptych with the Miracles of Christ. Detail of the left wing obverse, infra-red*

Pl. XXXVIII

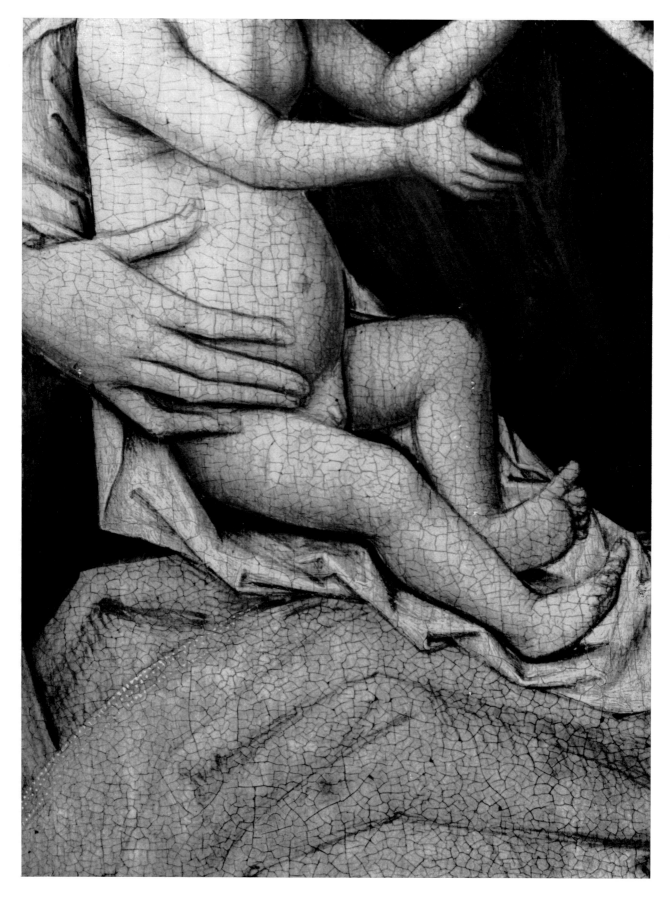

No. 131: Anonymous *(13), The Triptych with the Miracles of Christ. Detail of the left wing reverse, infra-red*

Pl. XXXIX

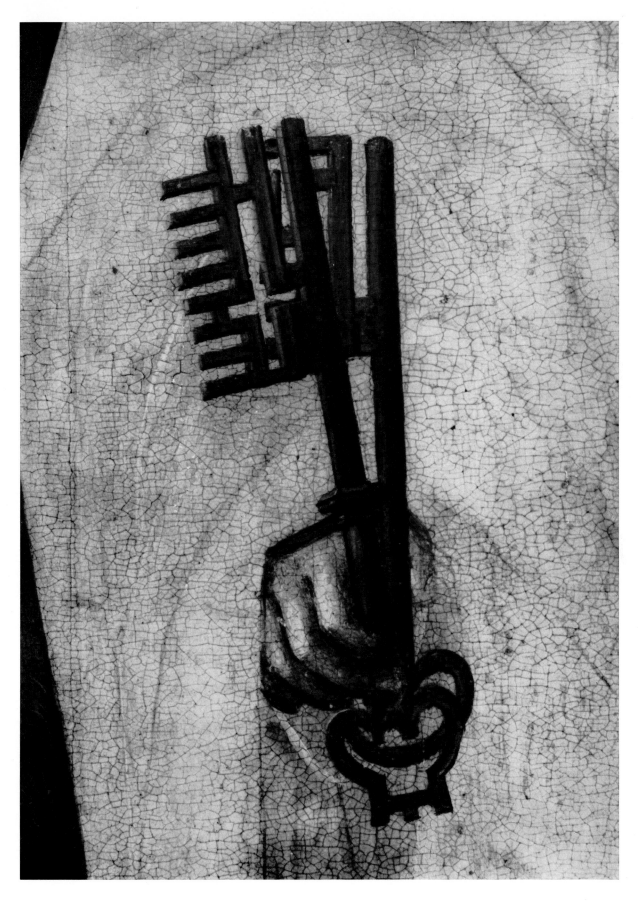

No. 131: Anonymous *(13), The Triptych with the Miracles of Christ. Detail of the right wing reverse, infra-red*

Pl. XL

No. 131: Anonymous *(13), The Triptych with the Miracles of Christ. Detail of the central panel, X-radiograph (1:1)*

Pl. XLI

No. 131: Anonymous *(13), The Triptych with the Miracles of Christ. Detail of the central panel, X-radiograph (1 : 1)*

Pl. XLII

No. 131: Anonymous (13), The Triptych with the Miracles of Christ. Detail of the left wing obverse, X-radiograph (1:1)

Pl. XLIII

No. 131: Anonymous *(13), The Triptych with the Miracles of Christ. Detail of the right wing obverse, X-radiograph (1:1)*

Pl. XLIV

No. 131: Anonymous (13), The Triptych with the Miracles of Christ. Detail of the left wing reverse, X-radiograph (1:1)

Pl. XLV

No. 131: Anonymous *(13), The Triptych with the Miracles of Christ. Detail of the right wing reverse, X-radiograph (1:1)*

Pl. XLVI

Mémoriaux of Antoine de Succa, Brussels, Bibliothèque Royale Albert Ier, f° 11
Michelle of France, John IV and Philip of Saint Pol, Dukes of Brabant

Pl. XLVII

*a) Charles the Bold, stained glass panel (now destroyed) of Notre-Dame, Bruges; b) Mary of Burgundy, and
c) Maximilian of Austria, stained glass panels from the Chapel of the Holy Blood, Bruges (London, Victoria and Albert Museum)*

Pl. XLVIII

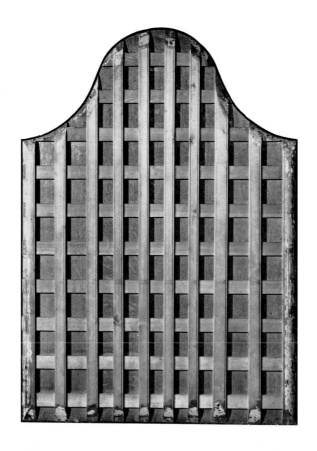

a) No. 131: Anonymous *(13), The Triptych with the Miracles of Christ. Central panel, the Reverse*
b) No. 133: Group Marmion *(4), The Virgin and Child at half-length. The Reverse*
c) No. 134: Group Memlinc *(15), The Man of Sorrows in the Arms of the Virgin. The Reverse*

Pl. XLIX

No. 132: Group Eyck *(9), The Madonna and the Child, after restoration*

Pl. L

No. 132: Group Eyck *(9), The Madonna and the Child, X-radiograph*

Pl. LI

No. 132: Group Eyck *(9), The Madonna and the Child, after cleaning and before restoration*

Pl. LII

No. 132: Group Eyck *(9), The Madonna and the Child, infra-red*
The photograph reveals a change in composition in the lower part of the robe at the opening of the mantle (A.P. and R.V.S.)

Pl. LIII

No. 132: Group Eyck (9), The Madonna and the Child. a) The Reverse; b) The right edge of the planed panel (M 10×)

Pl. LIV

No. 132: Group Eyck (9), The Madonna and the Child. a) The left edge, with the groove traced in the paint layer (M 15×);
b) The groove near the left edge and the still-life on the window-sill, after cleaning, in 1958 (M 5×).
Groove traced on a still soft preparation. This photograph also reveals important and localised wearing, often corresponding with ruptures in the paint layer, such as can be seen left of the foot of the pitcher. The glass on the window-sill (Pl. LVI) has disappeared during the cleaning that took away varnishes, overpainting and superficial retouching. This glass was in fact painted between two coats of varnish (A.P. and R.V.S.)

Pl. LV

No. 132: Group Eyck *(9), The Madonna and the Child. Bust of the Virgin and Child (M 2½×)*

Pl. LVI

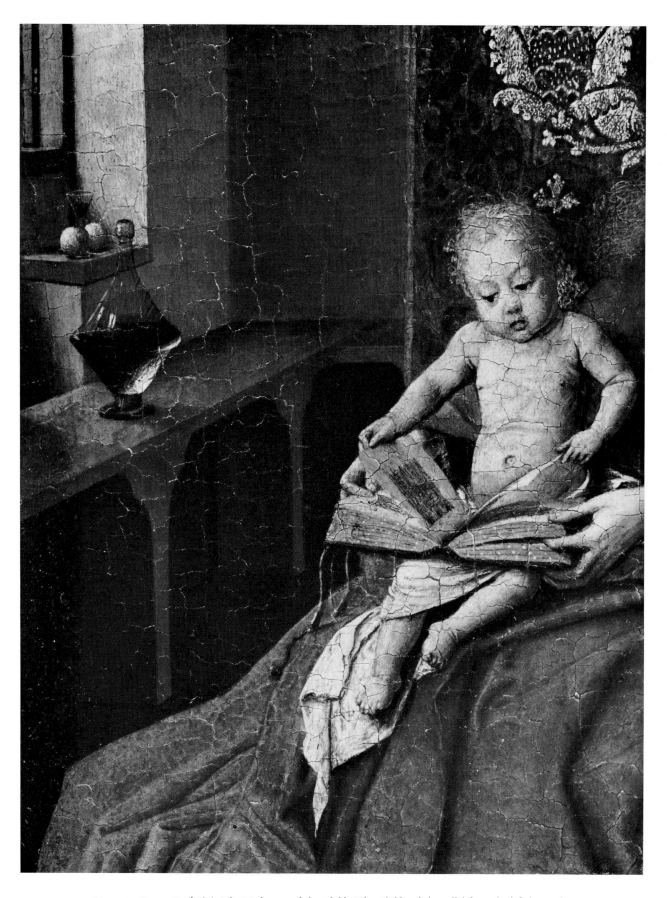

No. 132: Group Eyck *(9), The Madonna and the Child. The Child and the still-life on the left (M 2×)*

Pl. LVII

No. 132: Group Eyck *(9), The Madonna and the Child. The still-life, the cupboard and the right edge (M 2×)*

Pl. LVIII

No. 132: Group Eyck (9). *The Madonna and the Child. The lower left corner (M 2×).*
The forms are indicated by outlines but lack weight and volume; the edge of the red mantle seems to float in space (A.P. and R.V.S.).

Pl. LIX

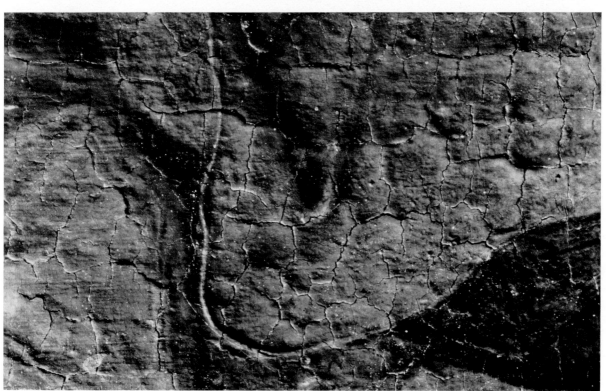

No. 132: Group Eyck (*9*), *The Madonna and the Child. a*) *Detail showing the folds in the Virgin's mantle* (M 5×);
b) *Detail showing the wooden floor and the carpet below the Virgin's mantle* (M 20×)
The pictorial execution lacks precision (A.P. *and* R.V.S.)

Pl. LX

No. 132: Group Eyck *(9), The Madonna and the Child.*
The inscription on the left after the removal of the transparent protein film (M 5×)
Crackles, wearing and overpainting (A.P. and R.V.S.)

Pl. LXI

No. 132: Group Eyck *(9), The Madonna and the Child. The inscription on the right (M 5×)*
The inscription is contemporary with the painting and equally weak in execution;
it is careless and without style (A.P. and R.V.S.)

Pl. LXII

No. 132: Group Eyck *(9), The Madonna and the Child.*
Detail showing the face of the Virgin with retouching strokes (M 20×)

Pl. LXIII

No. 132: Group Eyck *(9), The Madonna and the Child.*
Detail of the left part of the brocade hanging revealing, after cleaning, the transparent protein film (M 20 ×)
The shrinking of the protein film caused ruptures in the paint layer (A.P. and R.V.S.)

Pl. LXIV

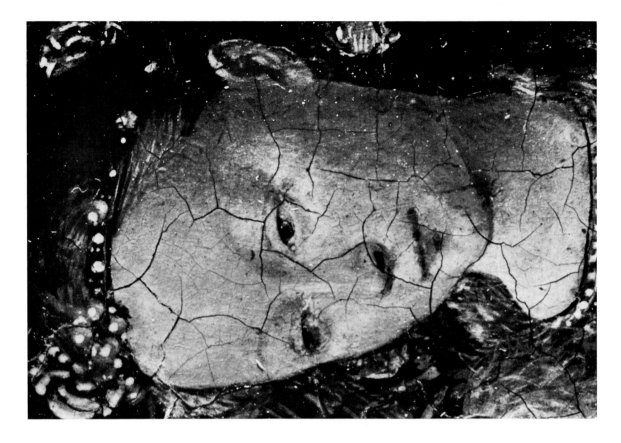

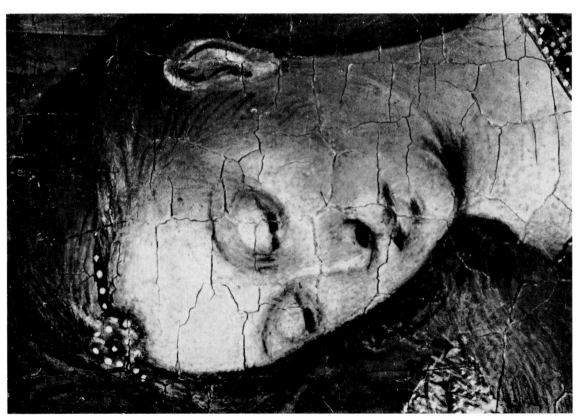

a) No. 132: Group Eyck (*9*), *The Madonna and the Child. The Virgin's head* (M 5×);
b) Jan van Eyck, triptych *The Virgin in the Church* (Dresden, Staatliche Kunstsammlungen). *The Virgin's head* (M 5×)

Pl. LXV

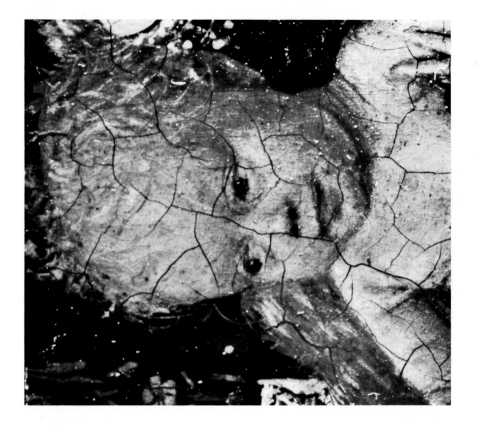

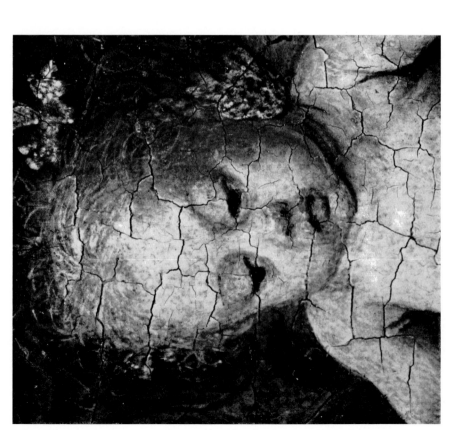

a) No. 132: Group Eyck (9). The Madonna and the Child. The Child's head (M 5×);

b) Jan van Eyck, triptych The Virgin in the Church (Dresden, Staatliche Kunstsammlungen). The Child's head (M 5×)

(*Pl. LXIV and LXV*) *Besides differences in material and crackling, the faces differ in aesthetic quality, as well as in expression. In the Dresden painting, the continuity of the glazes is the result of the fluidity of the material; in the Melbourne painting, the thickness of the pasta necessitated an application with short touches, hatched in order to maintain a certain transparency and to control the execution; this discontinuity in execution is best seen in the Virgin's face (A.P. and R.V.S.).*

Pl. LXVI

Group Eyck, *The Madonna and the Child (The "Verdura" Picture), private Collection, Rome*

Pl. LXVII

Van Eyck, *The Adoration of the Lamb (Ghent, Cathedral of S. Bavo), detail, X-radiograph (1:1)*
On this detail of the Holy Maidens, the modelling is built up in subtle gradations of density while in the Ince Hall Madonna, highlights only are present. In the former the thickness of the ground prevents the crackling from following the horizontal grain of the wood, but the network varies according to the pictorial structure, while in Melbourne the crackling is not related to this structure (A.P. and R.V.S.)

Pl. LXVIII

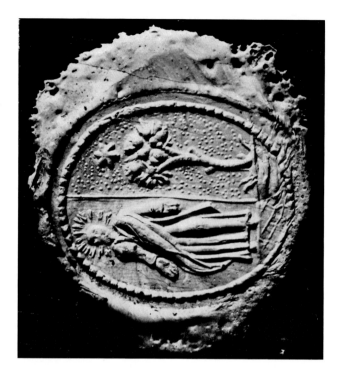

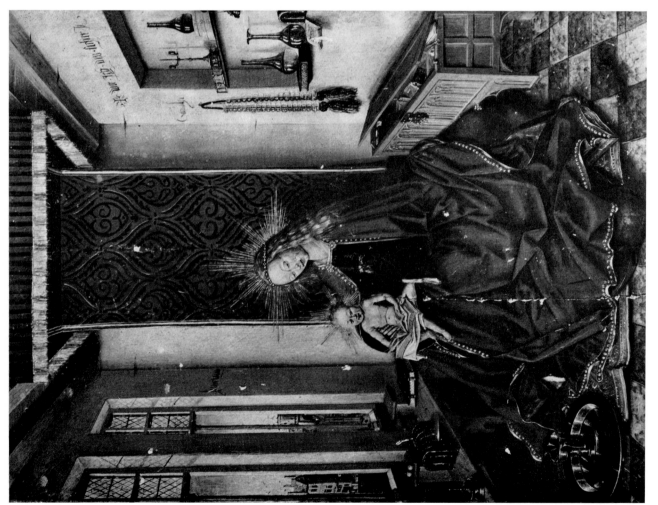

b) No. 132: Group Eyck (9), The Madonna and the Child.
Unidentified wax seal on the back of the panel (M 3× approx.)

a) Group Eyck, The Madonna and Child in a Room, Covarrubias, Collegiate Church

Pl. LXIX

No. 133: Group Marmion *(4), The Virgin and Child at half-length*

Pl. LXX

No. 133: Group Marmion *(4), The Virgin and Child at half-length, infra-red*

Pl. LXXI

No. 133: Group Marmion *(4), The Virgin and Child at half-length. Detail, X-radiograph (1:1)*

Pl. LXXII

No. 133: Group Marmion (4), The Virgin and Child at half-length. The upper half

Pl. LXXIII

No. 133: Group Marmion (4), The Virgin and Child at half-length. The lower half

Pl. LXXIV

No. 133: Group Marmion *(4), The Virgin and Child at half-length. The head of the Virgin (M* $1\frac{1}{2}\times$ *approx.)*

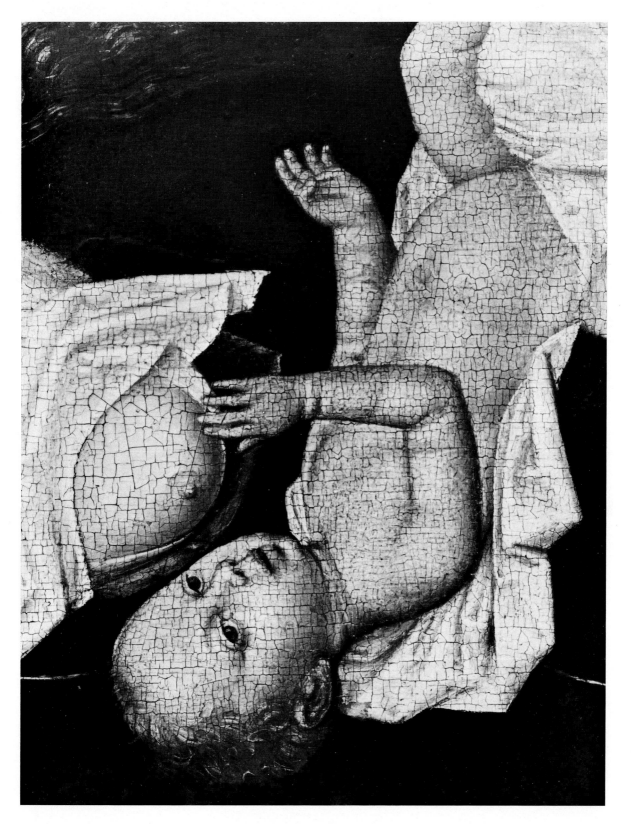

Pl. LXXV

No. 133: Group Marmion (4), The Virgin and Child at half-length. The Child (M 1½×approx.)

Pl. LXXVI

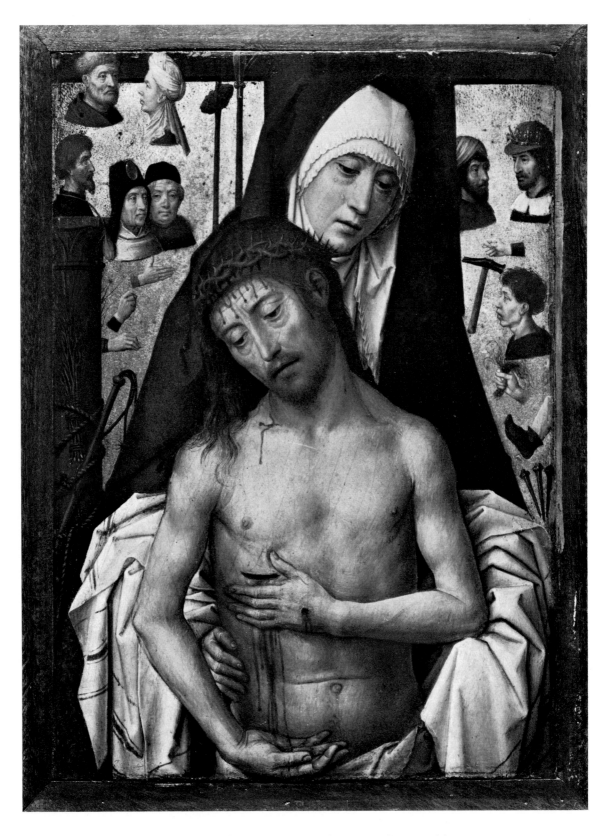

No. 134: Group Memlinc *(15), The Man of Sorrows in the Arms of the Virgin*

Pl. LXXVII A

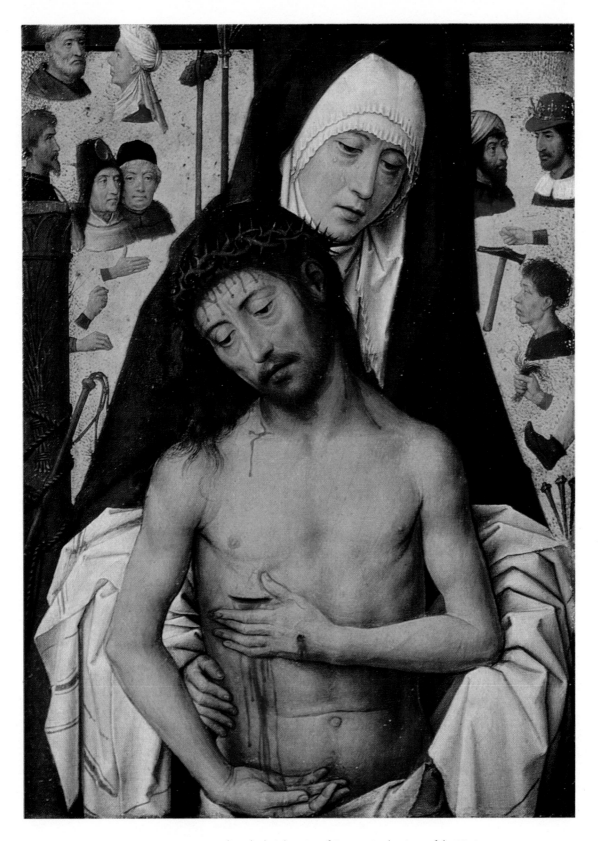

No. 134: Group Memlinc *(15), The Man of Sorrows in the Arms of the Virgin*

Pl. LXXVII

No. 134: Group Memlinc *(15), The Man of Sorrows in the Arms of the Virgin, infra-red*

Pl. LXXVIII

No. 134: Group Memlinc *(15), The Man of Sorrows in the Arms of the Virgin.*
Detail of Christ's hands, infra-red (M 1½ approx.)

Pl. LXXIX

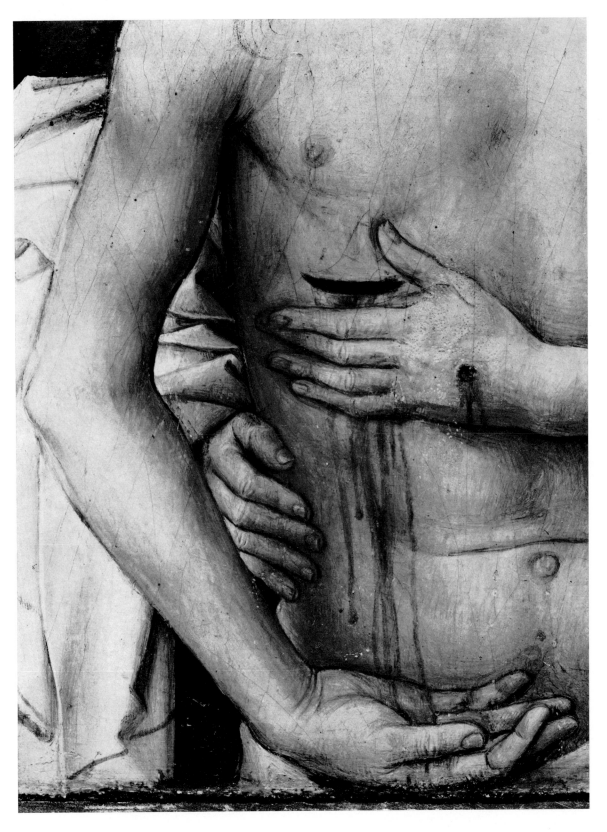

No. 134: Group Memlinc *(15), The Man of Sorrows in the Arms of the Virgin.
Detail of Christ's hands (M 1½ approx.)*

Pl. LXXX

Pl. LXXXI

No. 134: Group Memlinc (15), The Man of Sorrows in the Arms of the Virgin.   The lower half, X-radiograph (1:1)

Pl. LXXXII

No. 134: Group Memlinc *(15), The Man of Sorrows in the Arms of the Virgin. The upper left corner (M 2×)*

Pl. LXXXIII

No. *134:* Group Memlinc *(15), The Man of Sorrows in the Arms of the Virgin. The background at right (M 2×)*

Pl. LXXXIV

No. 134: Group Memlinc (15), The Man of Sorrows in the Arms of the Virgin. Christ and Virgin, detail (M 2×)

Printed by Erasmus S.A., Ledeberg/Ghent, Belgium
Dépot légal D/1971/0060/1 — 4ᵉ trimestre 1971
Printed in Belgium